Nine Lives

About the Author

A graduate of Trinity College Dublin, Dónal joined the Irish Department of Foreign Affairs in 1974. Since his retirement in 2015 he has acted as a mentor and consultant. He is a founder of a network of University of the Third Age (U3A) groups with over 450 members and has been a Board member of the European Movement. He recently resigned as Passport Appeals Officer, made under appointment from the Minister for Foreign Affairs.

Nine Lives

The Recollections
of a Dedicated Diplomat

Dónal Denham

The Liffey Press

Published by The Liffey Press Ltd
'Clareville', 307 Clontarf Road
Dublin D03 PO46, Ireland
www.theliffeypress.com

A catalogue record of this book is
available from the British Library.

ISBN 978-1-8383593-8-6

Printed in Ireland by SprintPrint.

Contents

Acknowledgements

With thanks, as ever, to the only true and constant love of my life, Siobhán, without whom nothing worthwhile would have happened to me, and whose contribution as an unpaid 'trailing spouse' was a treasure beyond measure, largely unrecognised by officialdom.

And to my children, Barry, Aisling, Andrea and Deirdre, whom I love dearly; what more could a father ask than to have a son who makes him proud and three beautiful daughters who make him so lucky as well as proud!

This book is dedicated to our grandchildren, Arpad and Audrey, and James who live in Melbourne, Australia, a lonely continent, too far away, and to all my future grandchildren, their legacy of my love.

I know that the first thing people do with an autobiography is to look in the index to see if they are mentioned; I apologise to any of my many friends if you are not there!

Dónal Denham
Ambassador of Ireland (retd.)
March 2022

Chapter 1

Growing Up, an Education
and First Posting to Paris

Growing up on Greenlea Road and the good life in Purley, Surrey;
back to college; meeting my bride at Mass; Terry Wogan at the BBC
and my only career move; our first European Presidency; Paris, a four-
year Lune de Miel; learning the trade from an old pro; bread, wine, and
boulevards; hospital morgues and prison cells; a day in consular life.

I am told I was delivered on 15 August 1950, in the confines of
the Lisieux Nursing Home, 7 Herbert Place, now a language
school, clocking in at seven pounds and that Maeve Hillery, President Hillery's spouse, and Rhoda McKitterick, Matron in Jervis
Street, were both present for this important occasion; presumably, they were providing back-up, just in case, as my mother
had had difficulty with previous pregnancies. My own version
of the story is that I was born on the Northside (where my parents were living at the time at 310 Howth Road, just up from St
Brigids) and either was kidnapped or escaped – depending on
whom I am talking to – to Greenlea Road, Terenure when I was
two years of age.

I was baptised some days later in St Andrew's Church, West-
land Row, as were so many baby Dubliners, gaining the middle

name of Mario in the process, to acknowledge my arrival on the Feast of the Assumption. At least I avoided the far more common middle name of Mary that so many Irish boys were then labelled with at birth, all in the cause of the Marian Year phenomenon. Few people know that the baptismal font in St. Andrews was part of the munificence and generosity of The Liberator, Daniel O'Connell. Apparently, he donated it along with two valuable paintings shortly after the Church was blessed in 1843. It is known by locals as the O'Connell Font and was originally a nineteenth century wine cooler; two handles and a tap were later removed. Sure, 'tis no wonder I am very partial to the red wine!

Terenure, 1952-1963

Greenlea, as our road was known, was an idyllic environment in which to grow up in allegedly grim 1950s' Ireland. I was privileged, I admit, being a spoilt, only son until I was nine when my lovely little sister, Caitriona, arrived. The shock of the new, and of a slightly disjointed nose (I broke it falling down the stone stairs of Terenure College Primary School a few months after she had appeared) soon wore off. Triona went on to live in almost perfect harmony with her big brother when we moved across the Irish Sea to Surrey. She subsequently qualified as a nurse, becoming a district nurse first in Charing Cross ICU, in at the deepest end, then in Somerset where she lived happily with her husband, Ian (an IT genius) and her three lovely children, Sinead, Jonathan and Jamie. Alas, Triona passed away from cancer at the age of 47, much to my eternal regret and deep, enduring sadness. And it was ironic that she had qualified as a specialist nurse providing care to people with cancer so that when she fell ill herself, there was no disguising the inevitable. She was such a good person; it shook my faith to the core when she was taken from us all.

Dublin was a safe environment, easy to traverse, whose boundaries had been well-established and with a sense of stability and continuity that is no longer assured. Deeply nostalgic and indulgent it may be, but early memories of crying my way through Mrs Owley's primary school off Fortfield Road, of literally leaping over the wall (yes, I did read the nun's story as a teen) to walk along by the lake up to 'College' (Terenure, the 'Nure') and of seemingly endless days spent out 'on the road' playing with neighbours, still fill my dreams. I also recall some very enjoyable 'snowy days' when the world seemed to pause, to realise the elemental nature of life on earth, a moment of shared silence.

I only discovered later that the first half of the road had been built in the 1940s and was largely occupied by the Jewish community of South Dublin. The Irish Jewish population had swelled to over 5,500 people in the early twentieth century as a result of many families fleeing eastern European pogroms. Many had settled in the immediate area of Rathgar and Terenure, near enough to walk to Walworth Road synagogue; such was the expansion then that a new synagogue was built and opened in Terenure in 1953. And it came as a belated revelation many years later that one of my good friends on the road of that time, Stewart Segal, was the child of a Holocaust survivor's family; his mother, Doris lost her parents and siblings to the Holocaust, a terrible tragedy that we should never forget or diminish.

It was also years later before I understood the true obscene significance of what had been done to the European Jewish community during WWII. As Consul General in San Francisco, I met with the American Jewish Committee there and faced their ire at how little Ireland had done as a society to face up to the genocide that the Nazis had carried out, crimes against humanity made explicit by the 1945 Nuremberg War Crimes Tribunal. De Valera's signature of the Book of Condolences for Hitler in 1945 is something, as an Irish diplomat, I particularly regret.

I hope I made some personal atonement later on during my time as Ambassador to Lithuania, which was the original source country for many of the Jewish families in Ireland, and which had seen 96 per cent of the Jewish population, the largest percentage of any country, wiped out by the Holocaust. Indeed, despite the commemorative work of the Holocaust Education Trust Ireland and, more recently, of Holocaust Awareness Ireland under Oliver Sears, himself a second generation Holocaust survivor, we in Ireland have little or no appreciation of the true horrors of the genocide of the Jewish population in Eastern Europe during that time.

Thanks to my close friend Dr Dovid Katz, Professor of Yiddish Studies at Oxford and latterly at the University of Vilnius, I hosted a diplomatic reception in June 2008, attended by a large number of my diplomatic colleagues to honour Fania Brankovsky, then 85 years of age, a teenager during the Holocaust and a Vilnius ghetto survivor to boot.

Fania lost both her parents and her only sister when the ghetto was purged without warning in 1943 by the Nazis, who occupied Vilnius, and their collaborators. Fania escaped to the forest through a sewage drain and made her way to a hidden partisan camp where she joined the freedom fighters and fought both German and local Fascist elements from 1943 to 1945.

At the time of our event, I was made aware that Fania was being investigated by the Lithuanian police due to anonymous allegations made against her for those activities. Our collective diplomatic gesture of solidarity with Fania was one of the high-lights of my career and something I shall never forget.

So, to resume my narrative, Greenlea and 1950's Dublin meant playing on the road with a huge gang of friends of all ages, shapes and persuasions and both sexes, lots of ride-on toys, my first bikes, penny ice-pops in summer, comic books galore every week and month (*Jack & Jill, Dandy, Beano, Lion, Tiger, Eagle, Classics Illustrated, War Picture Library*), lots of adventures with Roy of the Rovers and Dan Dare, Pilot of the Future! By the time we left Greenlea, I had a veritable treasure trove of children's weeklies, monthlys and annuals, all of which, alas, were left behind when we moved to England in 1963. I hope some child, somewhere, is enjoying that amassed collection!

Spoilt as I was, I also had the finest, well-used Dinky car collection on the entire road! Again, they disappeared into a suit-case which I foolishly gave, on permanent loan as it turns out, to the younger brother of a friend of mine. I suppose it *is* too late to ask for them back?

Toys and comics certainly bought an amount of juvenile friendship, but I like to think that it was more than material possessions that has kept at least one such relationship intact and occasionally nurtured, for example, with the Tobin family. Their mother, Carmel, was like a second mother to me and her daughter, Nuala, and her spouse, Paddy, are still lifelong good friends.

As already mentioned, we used to have a few days of decent snow in winter in the 1950s, school was abandoned and snowball fights to beat the band. In summer, it was day trips to sunny

Dollymount (my favourite, soft blond sand underfoot, warmish waters, playing in The Wreck – I still don't know which wooden hull that ship was), to Seapoint (cold and rocky) occasionally to Killiney (always too stony) and, rarely, to Portmarnock or the Hole in the Wall at Sutton (foreign territory, Southern passports in hand!). Holidays in Donabate where the dunes and the crabs were amazing! Imagine, one could drive in those days on those pristine beaches without any regard for the environmental damage we were causing!

I recall the Corona fizzy drink salesman calling regularly to deliver a really red pop, orange and lemonade flavours, too, please. And the inimitable black and white, really fuzzy, TV arriving in the late 1950s when, on a late Saturday afternoon, the entire young neighbourhood gathered around our Bush (or was it Pye – names to conjure with!) box-like TV set, tiny grey screen aglow, to watch Clayton Moore shout 'High Ho, Silver … away!' to the tune of the William Tell Overture in yet another episode of *The Lone Ranger* and his constant 'Red Indian' companion, Tonto, played by Jay Silverheels. Oh, the memories! *Robin Hood*, riding through the glen, *On Safari*, with Armand and Mikaela Denis, *The Count of Monte Cristo*, and, at an early age, Jack & Jill, Sooty & Sweep, Noddy, Andy Pandy, Bill & Ben and their flower-pot companion, 'Lil weed'! Zootime with Johnny Morris, Muffin the Mule … the list is endless and totally self-indulgently nostalgic!

On a more serious note, early television was also the 1956 failed revolution in Hungary, sinister Soviet tanks moving through the centre of Budapest and, in 1959, Harold Macmillan resigning, Rab Butler, Quentin Hogg (Lord Hailsham) and Ian McCloud fighting it out to succeed him and the reluctant eventual winner, Sir Alec Douglas-Home, emerging from the High

Tory shadows; it was the first time I heard of smoke-filled rooms. The wheel turns: the Tory party doesn't seem to have learnt any lessons from Brexit about leadership conspiracies.

There was also the 'Profumo Affair' which, whenever mentioned on the television, UK channels only, in my presence led to the off switch being immediately activated. But my parental censors didn't reckon on my tenacity when interest is piqued and the easy access to British scandal sheets brought into the home by my newspaper-loving father. A daily feature throughout his all-too-brief life (of which more later) was his arrival home with at least one plastic bag full of newspaper and media trade publications which I devoured. Newspapers may be dying rapidly but they will never be forgotten while I am around.

Life in those days revolved around *The Irish Press, The Sunday Press* (hard to believe it was the largest-selling newspaper of its day), *The Evening Press* and later on, when Dad moved with Douglas Gageby, his close friend, to *The Irish Times* in 1959, it was that paper of record plus *The Irish Field*, the *Radio Review*, the *Sunday Review*, the latter pioneers of the tabloid format and precursors of the *Sunday World* and *RTÉ Guide*.

The demise of that grand old evening paper, *The Evening Mail*, after a brief, desperate, humiliating and ultimately unsuccessful conversion from broadsheet to tabloid was one of the sadder moments in Irish media history. Technically 'suspended', it ceased publication in 1962 and brought to an end that treasured, almost incomprehensible phrase beloved of the street-corner 'newsboys' and shouted with gusto to passersby: 'Heralomail! Heralomail!'

One of my most enduring memories from those days was when my father was despatched to the *Irish Press* London office for a six-month stint in 1957. I will never forget the kerosene-laden excitement that my first visit to the beautiful art deco Collinstown air terminal generated, or the pure thrill of stepping up the small stairs to board an Aer Lingus DC 3. The steep slant of the aisle, the small square porthole windows, the shudder and judder of those piston engines, enveloped in a thick cloud of smoke as the magnetos began to fire and the blades slowly rotated. It is still my all-time favourite aeroplane. I had the good fortune to relive some of those magical moments again while in Helsinki in 2015 on a preserved Finnair DC3.

Waves from the ground staff, a short, bumpy back-wheel taxi out to the runway, the sudden, deafening increase in engine noise, followed by the exhilaration of the G force as we trundled down the runway for what seemed like forever, a gradual straightening of the plane as the tail wheel lifted off and there we were … flying! What a lucky lad I was to have that privilege so young!

London in those days was living in Mrs Eileen Kilgallon's B&B in Regent's Park after a few weeks in The Irish Club in Eaton Square, then a luxurious accommodation in a fabulous location, sadly no longer with us. Life there was punctuated by frequent visits to the park's boating lake. 'Come in Number 7!' was a frequently heard hail as we delighted in paddling our little coracle or pedallo around among the lazy, idle ducks. And, if I behaved, I secured the reward of a visit to Hamley's treasure-laden toy shop on Regent Street or to Selfridges world-famous emporium, frequently returning with suits of armour or six-gun and holster and other such militaria which provided our amusement in those days. I still have a photo of myself dressed up in a knight's helmet with mail to prove it. And remember, I have admitted to being spoilt as a kid!

Feeding the pigeons in Trafalgar Square was also popular. I loved travelling on London's buses, many of them pre-war Leyland double-deckers, and particularly the ubiquitous London trolley bus which hissed and sparked, and especially in the wet weather there was the sinister, sooty smell and dark marvel of the Tube. 'Mind the doors please, mind the doors!' But invariably it was the people occasionally caught in them who needed minding! And, on important occasions, when Mum insisted and Dad gave in, we guiltily caught the occasional iconic black cab. I recall in those days that much of London still bore the open wounds of the Blitz. Bomb sites piled with rubble and other decaying materials remained amid still standing structures, like gaps among teeth.

Other memories are of the old Science Museum, full of ancient steam engines and other relics of nineteenth century Victorian engineering prowess; of afternoons watching *Brains Trust, Liberace* with his glittery tight-fitting suits, large collars zipped down to show a hairy chest, and candelabra atop his white grand piano; and later, *What's My Line* and *This is Your Life* with Eamonn Andrews, *Double Your Money*, Hughie Green, and *Open the Box* with Michael Miles. I enjoyed that all-too-brief sojourn in London.

I was just getting used to life in Terenure College Senior School (for example, Father Grace, who delighted in getting the class to hold hands in a circle for our first-ever physics lesson then passing an electric current around us; I never recovered from the literal shock and physics became the one subject I never passed in any exam) when Dad came home one evening and announced that we were packing up and leaving for London again, this time permanently. That was July 1963.

Purley, Surrey, 1963–1970

So I left Greenlea life behind, with great sadness, both at the break in friendships and, as I soon discovered at the other end, alas too late, the ever-lasting loss of my fine, now rare, collection both of comic books and Dinky toys which mysteriously disappeared en route to England. I realise, of course, that parenting isn't easy and that difficult decisions must be taken on occasion.

However, I have to say that life in the leafy suburb of Sanderstead, Surrey, just 10 miles south of the Thames and with the shopping magnet of Croydon within a short bus ride, was beyond my wildest dreams. It was 'practically perfect in every way'. We had a detached house, parks and the local library within walking distance, and school was reached either by bus or train, both still exciting to use in those days. And the climate seemed milder, always nice sunny days in summer with gold and red leaf colours in autumn. I was allowed to have a Collie dog, Rory, who was a delight to take for an evening walk.

My second sister, Grainne, was born in July 1964, a miracle baby for my mother at nearly 40 years of age, after losing a daughter at birth in 1952 (I only discovered this a couple of years ago, by accident; neither Mum nor Dad let on). Grainne was herself to lose a child, Killian, a twin, to leukaemia at 9 years of age; her story of resilience in that adversity is in itself a worthy narrative (more in Chapter 7). Triona and Grainne went to school at the elegant and sought-after St Anne's College, a convent school run by nuns in large wimples, at the end of Sanderstead Road. I served Mass there, followed by a delicious cooked breakfast which made the frosty early morning starts bearable. Best of all, my own school, John Fisher at Purley, turned out to be among the best years of my life, full of good friendships, great teachers (no hanky-panky evident at all), interesting lessons and rugby played on the school pitches located on what was once London's first airport, Croydon!

In the summer of 1965, my doting parents arranged a French exchange for me; it was all the rage to swap families with a French equivalent although in this case I went to France first and Alain, my French counterpart who lived in Lourdes, in deepest southern France amid the Pyrenees, came to us the following year. I flew to Paris Orly and changed planes all on my own, without any problem; a beautiful Air France ground hostess did the needful at Orly. My flight down to Lourdes was eventful for two reasons. I travelled on an Air France Caravelle, then on the cutting edge of jet plane travel, a fabulously 'chic' looking aircraft. And secondly, just as we approached the Alps, we flew through a massive thunderstorm that tossed us up and down and around like a kite! I became good friends with a lovely American lady sitting beside me.

There were no mobiles and hardly any landlines in those days. My parents had conducted all the arrangements, including the date and time of my arrival, via written correspondence. I had a name and telephone number for my exchange family on a piece of paper but nothing more. Fortunately, the American lady had volunteered to remain with me until I was picked up by Alain's father (he turned out to be a widower with a gorgeous girlfriend). I waited and waited but no one stepped forward in the small, provincial arrivals hall of Lourdes airport. Eventually, my new-found US saviour took me to her posh hotel in downtown Lourdes and booked me a separate room. A call to Alain's number elicited no reply. I spent a restless, sleepless night.

The next morning, after several attempts, the number I had was finally answered. Alain's father had no English, but we muddled through enough that he finally appeared at the hotel at lunchtime and promptly took me for my first (of many) Pastis at a local hostelry. I barely had a chance to thank my US guardian angel and have never managed to find her since. She was certainly part of my miracle of Lourdes!

Over our second or third Pastis, I managed to work out that Alain's father was a souvenir seller, with a converted Peugeot 404 station wagon whose rear was taken up with tray upon tray of all sizes of plastic Virgin Marys, filled with 'holy Lourdes water' which he replenished from his local water tap! There was also a myriad of Marian snow globes and the like. He peddled these all over the villages of the Pyrenees and had been away overnight on such a trip, having confused the date of my arrival – or so he claimed. I always suspected Guy, for that was his name, had his own way of calculating time!

The rest of my notional time in Lourdes was spent hurtling around precipitous bends in the mountains to rival the best of the Monte Carlo Rally drivers, or camping at the coast, or learning about mushroom picking and drinking local wines, with intervals in between spent at their residence beside 'Lac de Lourdes' where Guy maintained a nightclub disco on the side. It was my first experience of ultraviolet strobe lighting!

I did write to my parents to tell them I was safe and sound and happy with my exchange arrangements; I omitted the bits about the see-saw flight and the delayed welcome. Nor did I mention that a visit to the Marian Grotto was not on my daily itinerary, although I did manage to offload more than a few plastic statues on our Alpine travels. And what happened in the nightclub stayed in the nightclub. 'Twas a glorious, riotous summer, never to be forgotten.

The return journey for Alain was much more mundane.

I could wax lyrical about the pleasures of growing up in 1960's London, an age of generational and cultural revolution, political change – Harold Wilson, George Brown and Bernadette McAliskey Devlin – and sexual liberation, but it will have to await Volume 2 of these memoirs!

I was both lucky and privileged to attend the John Fisher School, Peak's Hill, Purley, a Roman Catholic independent grammar school within walking distance of where we lived in Sanderstead. And I was proud to be chosen as Captain of the third XV, those who enjoyed their rugby if not particularly good at playing it, and of achieving 10 GCE O-levels and, eventually, 3 GCE A-levels, in French, History and English (especially boastful of my A grade!), and of gaining a place at Trinity College Dublin in History and Political Science which brought me 'home' to Dublin. But leaving John Fisher School behind has not been easy. Those idyllic days are never far from my daydreams.

I will never forget the wonderful priests who taught us, especially a proud Scot, Father Ian MacDonald, who instilled, with his own brilliant classroom approach, a life-long love of History, the formidable Father Fuchs for Classics, the mild Father Kensington for an introduction to Edith Piaf and all that the best of France represented and, not least, Father Fawcett, a quintessential Englishman, who encouraged fair play, on and off the rugby pitch, and cemented my faith in Roman Catholicism, despite all the temptations and doubts that arose during my school days living in a post-religious society. And Mr Derek Enright, who later went on to become Labour MP for North Yorkshire, who rolled his own black tobacco cigarettes in class (believe it or not!) and who perfected in us the skills of public debating. He had an uncanny ability to attract some high-profile politicians of the time to visit us at the Society for the Encouragement of Culture, Arts & Science (SECAS), the portentously named sixth-form school debating club, of which I became President in my turn). Another character from that era was Mr John Treacy, our sixth form English teacher who spent all his spare time in West Belfast and who regaled us in class in 1968/69 with his experiences of the Burntollet Bridge Civil Rights march and beyond, to the extent that we reached the end of the year having covered very little of the A-Level curriculum! I remember vividly his slim, tobacco-stained fingers as he held up some book or other.

I am still in touch with my best friend from the John Fisher School, Paddy Hamlin, and his spouse, Trish; I am even a delinquent godfather to his daughter, Katrina, who lives in Hong Kong and whom I intend to visit one of these days – high on the bucket list.

I ended up doing a further year in Cambridge Tutors in South Croydon, source of a life-long friendship with the inimitable John Burridge, he of a red, unreliable but superb MG TD and a fondness for quoting Winnie the Pooh! John was great company, one of nature's finest gentlemen, and I regret that our friendship has been much abused by neglect on my part. Again, a visit to Suffolk and beyond is on that same list.

I fell in love with my French teacher there, but unlike Emmanuel Macron, I never pursued her.

It was also a time, even back then, of racial intolerance, Little Britainism, Enoch Powell's Rivers of Blood remarks and incitement to hatred of immigrants. I am not surprised, therefore, by the Brexit xenophobic backlash. The UK was ever an Empire based on bigotry and prejudice.

For all that, I still get a great, nostalgic thrill out of my memories of life in the southeast. Of the Battle of Britain sites at close by Biggin Hill and Kenly, of holidays home in Ireland and a blissful family existence which included the joys of reading voraciously in lovely, book-scented libraries, of the simple pleasure of walking the Downs, of riding lessons and of discovering girls. Seven years in Sanderstead went by far too quickly! Some days, I wish I had never left!

Trinity College Dublin, 1970-74

I had an offer of a university place from Manchester University and from Goldsmiths in London, but my preferred choice was to return to Ireland to read History and Political Science at the University of Dublin, Trinity College. I have to say that even on a generous English grant, as they were in those days, my four years in Trinity College wasn't all it was cracked up to be.

I recall the Provost welcoming 'Freshers' in 1970, explaining that there were far more Roman Catholics in the university than its image would suggest, and despite 'the ban' imposed by John Charles McQuaid, RC Archbishop of Dublin and a close acquaintance of Eamon de Valera.

McQuaid in his day was one of the most influential persons in Irish politics, a major contributor to our still extant 1937 Constitution, a Jansenist Conservative. I am pleased to say the ban was lifted in 1970, although coming from the UK it didn't impinge on my sensibilities when applying to college.

I found Trinity cliquish, with old school chums sticking together and outsiders like myself struggling to break into college society; I believe this may still be true of Irish university life. My class of about 30 comprised a 'mixum-gatherem' of individuals which included the likes of one of the six 'Miss Fitts', daughters of then West Belfast SDP MP, Gerry Fitt; Hillery Simms, daughter of Church of Ireland Archbishop of Armagh, George Otto Simms; Michael Good, from South Africa who went on to achieve minor RTÉ celebrity status as a reporter in Belfast; Des Murphy, who became a barrister; and Dr Ciaran Brady, who went on to become Professor of Modern History in TCD. My closest friend, however, was Philip Grey who went on to a notable teaching and rugby coaching career, first in The King's Hospital School and later as Headmaster in Kilkenny College, to be felled in mid-career by a dreadful cycling accident.

Our lecturers over the four years were, in History, Professors Theodore Moody, first appointed over 30 years previously in 1939; Aidan Clarke, son of the poet; Jocelyn Otway-Ruthven, also known as The Ott; James Lydon; Christine Meek; Helga the Hammer Hammerstein; and my two favourites, David Thornley and Louis Cullen. For Political Science, a much drier experience than anticipated, we had Basil Chubb and the charismatic Patrick Keatinge. Professor Moody, then in charge of the History faculty, set the tone with an extremely distant approach to student relations. But my admiration for Professor Chubb has been high ever since I learned much later that he had served with distinction as an RAF pilot during WWII, something he never mentioned.

And prowling around campus in hat, scarf and ancient tweed coat, whatever the weather, was the inimitable R.B. McDowell. A.A. Luce was Senior Fellow, already at a great age then and hardly ever seen, even by his Philosophy students, and the noisy

Kerryman, Brendan Kennelly, was a Proctor, whatever that meant.

I joined 'the Hist', the College Historical Society, and watched the great Joe Revington in action many a week and a commanding Donel Deeney in the Chair. Mary Harney honed her political skills in public debate there, too, and we formed a friendship which has endured neglect!

I found college somewhat disappointing at an academic level, quite dull in the traditional approach the History faculty had adopted, despite early promise and one or two active lecturers, with smaller-format seminars only introduced in the latter two years of our course. And we were not cohesive at class level, with a large minority of students from Northern Ireland who tended to shun life in Dublin, local Dublin students who stuck together, and a spectrum of others, including myself, who craved inclusion but never quite achieved it.

So after four years I had few class friends to show for it. But TCD did stand out for three reasons: first and foremost, it introduced me to the love of my life, my biggest fan and harshest critic, my companion of over 40 years, Siobhán. It is true that our marriage was, nearly, made in Heaven. In fact, it began at daily Mass in No. 4, Front Square.

To explain: Father Brendan Heffernan had been appointed the first Catholic Chaplain of TCD in 1971, taking up residence over the Coffee Shop in No. 27. The College Chapel was still in Protestant hands in those days and it took over two years to have it reformed as an ecumenical venue. In the meantime, Mass quickly outgrew No. 27 and moved to the attic of No. 4. I offered my services to set up and take down the altar and so on. Siobhán was recruited as a reader; she had an amazing voice and beautiful brown eyes. After about a year, I took up the courage to ask her out, only to be rebuffed with a curt, 'No!'

A year later, I ended up on an outing to Glenmalure with Siobhán, Caoimhin O'Laoi and Yvonne MacDonagh in the back seat of Father Brendan's blue Opel. The rest is history, as they say. This period in college was also when Siobhán and I made a life-long friendship with a remarkable person, Soline Vatinel as she then was, a young French woman, later taking her mother's family name of Humbert (a famous French naval family name with Irish connections!). Soline went on to marry Colm Holmes, son of a distinguished Irish Ambassador and grandnephew of Harry Nicolls, the only Trinity undergraduate to participate in 1916 on the rebel side! I digress. Shortly after we met Soline, she confessed to feeling a strong calling from God, which both terrified and thrilled her. Soline had a vocation to be a priest, I am in no doubt of that.

Both she and her spouse, Colm, have fought hard, within the bounds and without, for reform of the institutional, doggedly clerical Roman Catholic church for women priests and for married priests. It is now happening as I write; the pity is that it is too little, too late. The institutional church is all but moribund. But our friendship has endured, despite our peripatetic lifestyle. Soline, Colm and Eamonn McCarthy, the first RC Assistant Chaplin in TCD, have visited us in our foreign postings and we meet up regularly when at home. Soline came home to Paris when we were there and we became good friends with her Dad, someone who knew his cheese and his wine and wasn't reluctant to share same. Likewise, Eamonn is in the annals of Denham diplomatic history as having led a student group of twelve in his precious but capricious Volkswagen van to visit us and the sites in Paris. The van broke down, as was its wont, and we had a large number of unscheduled house guests in our two-bed apartment … those were the days. You can imagine the strain that put on nineteenth-century French plumbing!

The second reason I enjoyed college was David Thornley and his enthusiasm for his classes in early twentieth century Irish history. He encouraged us to discuss our subject in detail and with passion. He was a sad loss to Irish politics. The 1973 general election was my first experience of participating in a political campaign, in his constituency of Dublin North West. It was hard fought, and he clung on to his seat, the last, in a tight battle with Fianna Fáil.

The final reason college was rewarding was for the formation of the Vincent de Paul conference there, in 1972, at the request of Father Heffernan who approached six of us to take it on: Brian O'Malley, our first President (he is now Finance Director of the national organisation); Joe Maguire, Treasurer; Bernie Nolan; Caoimhin and Yvonne and myself (Secretary).

Our early involvement was in the parish of St Andrew's where, as I said, I had been baptised. It is real 'auld' Dublin at its best. The St. Andrews Resource Centre there, which is a mainstay of the parish even now, owes its development to the student involvement of TCD. Diarmuid McCarthy, distinguished former Secretary General of the Department of the Taoiseach, took over from me as SVP President the year I graduated, and should be credited with forging that close and enduring link.

And I am humbled to understand that the SVP is now among the largest of undergraduate organisations in that august institution founded by Elizabeth I, Regina, in 1594!

I was so lucky to be chosen as one of 30, on graduation in 1974, to join the Department of Foreign Affairs as a Third Secretary out of the many hundreds who applied. I was one of only three or four in my class who went straight from college into the workforce. But I always seemed to have been fortunate when it came to gainful employment.

Meanwhile, our whirlwind romance continued. Engaged formally at Trinity Ball in May 1973, I completed my degree in 1974 and helped Siobhán with hers; I learnt a lot about Biochemistry in a relatively short time! We could have been the first Roman Catholic wedding in college, but Fleming family pressure meant it would take place at the Dominican Priory in Athy, County Kildare, also a first. That entailed complex negotiations, including a letter from the Archbishop to the local parish priest, Father Rogan, to enforce our decision of the Priory location.

We got married on 7 December 1974, a date that has always been easy to recall by its association with another 'Day of Infamy', the bombing of Pearl Harbour on that date in 1941. My Best Man was the inimitable Desmond Stark of Sutton, County Dublin, a true gent and scholar who enjoys splitting his life between Dublin and Rome. I met Des through Father Brendan, who officiated that day, and also via Geraldine Clarke, a mutual close friend in college. Geraldine went on to pursue a phenomenally successful career as a solicitor to the stars (and to the Denhams, so beware!), serving a term with distinction as President of the Law Society of Ireland, and to marry Eric Falkiner, former Junior Dean in college, and eminent microbiologist. Both Geraldine and Eric, together with their two delightful daughters, have been life-long friends ever since.

To digress a moment: during my first summers in Trinity, I worked, firstly, as a cellar man in the newly opened Royal Dublin Hotel, entrusted with the keys to the cellar and all the booze within – and no, I didn't abuse the responsibility – then as Library Assistant in The Irish Times Library, where the bios of all and sundry Irish gentry were kept on file under the supervision of the Library & Archives supervisor, Tony Lennon, a nice gent who passed away far too young. Under his close supervision I updated and carefully preserved individual obituary texts and refiled them, to await their respective deaths!

My most amazing summer job by far, however, believe it or not, was at the great British Broadcasting Corporation, the BBC or Beeb as it was affectionately known, at its iconic, art deco Portland Place headquarters, obtained by pure fluke. I recall being in a state of quiet desperation in May 1973 as I faced into a summer at home in the southeast of England without any source of funds to tide me over the long break; in those days, Trinity had the luxury of three seven-week terms, Michaelmas, Hilary and Trinity, with a four-month gap between the end and start of the academic year.

In desperation, I wrote to the Beeb to see if they took on temporary staff. In an answer to my fervent prayer I received a polite affirmative letter and application form. Within two weeks, I was happily ensconced in Central Services of the BBC, in charge of a 'Heavy Gang' of 16 sturdy, intimidating Cockneys who were responsible for moving anything and everything beyond a teacup and saucer from one studio to another across London. You wanted a grand piano for 'Friday Night is Music Night'? No problem, madam, call the Heavy Gang Scheduler (me). You wanted broadcast equipment delivered to Wimbledon for the

Tennis? Call HGS Denham. Or an orchestra suite of instruments? Call Denham.

Mind you, I often felt caught between a rock and a hard place, with impossibly short-notice demands:

> 'Er, sorry, old chap, we forgot you need a concert harp for Beethoven's Fifth tonight; any chance you could find one somewhere and pop it in a lorry and send it to the Royal Albert? (as in Hall)?'

To be balanced against death threats from my erstwhile teammates:

> 'Eh, mate, you f…ing schedule us for a half-hour lift and carry from Bush 'ouse to The Langham with those effing pianos ever again and we'll be coming round the other side of this counter!'

This was a reference to my only protection, a frail but tall wooden counter beyond which they had to stand to get their orders for the day and to report back each night, the dreaded end to every day!

On the other hand, I had complete control over the reservation and allocation of all BBC Conference Rooms which made for some interesting on-the-job visits to the innards of Portland Place, as well as responsibility for booking accommodation for those announcers working on late-night programmes. And I had control of overnight accommodation at The Langham Hotel nearby, then owned by the BBC and location of The BBC Club.

All in all, it was a fun job with lots of little nuggets to be enjoyed; Terry Wogan played a couple of requests for me and we had a chat over early morning coffees once or twice. He was, without doubt, as nice as the image he portrayed. I was also appreciated, and invited back during Christmas, Easter and final summer breaks to continue where I had left off. I even made enquiries about the possibilities of a career in the BBC, but it was not to be.

Meanwhile, our whirlwind romance flourished.

Department of Foreign Affairs (DFA), 1974-76

Siobhán, a great believer in etiquette and with Mrs Begley (her etiquette and social graces tutor at school) as her patron saint of good manners, sent out our wedding invitations before I had even graduated! Her confidence in my getting through the interview process for Foreign Affairs was not misplaced, I am relieved to say, and my first, rather intimidating day on the job was 28 October 1974. I was one of Garret (Fitzgerald's) Group, recruited beyond the traditional Irish Civil Service talent pool; I was one of an even more select number sourced from outside the Republic that year.

In those days, coffee at 11.00 in the so-called Civil Service Dining Club at the rear of Iveagh House was *de riguer*. It also seemed that only DFA types went to it and tables were graded according to rank. I knew I was in trouble when the Head of Human Resources approached where I was sitting with two other new entrants, Justin Harmon and Eugene Hutchinson, and then proceeded to ignore us to ask another colleague how his Dad, a Revenue Commissioner as it turned out, was keeping. So began 40 years of inner and outer circles in the DFA!

A posting to the Trade Aid Section, a new unit within the Economic Division, followed. The Economic Division looked after everything that wasn't either Political or Anglo-Irish, and its main focus was on our new membership of the European Economic Community.

The first Irish presidency began on 1 January 1975, less than three months after I had begun work. There was no Training Section in those days and, therefore, no training, despite the generous initial salary on offer (no, not exceptional; incomes were rising fast in Ireland in the 1970s, both in the private and public sectors).

Our induction consisted of a stern lecture from the Deputy Head of Personnel, Sean Guilfoyle, on the evils of drink which he assured us was lavishly bestowed on diplomatic personnel by one another. Sean was a general service officer of the old school, a perfect gent.

This was followed by a brief but entirely friendly encounter with Liam Rigney, Head of Personnel, again a lovely, decent individual with great compassion. Sadly, to my mind, these qualities were in shorter supply once Liam had moved on (he was rewarded with being appointed Ambassador to Denmark after his long, distinguished and heroic stint in HR), but more of that anon. Indeed, our family have reason to be eternally grateful to Liam and his good nature. When our eldest daughter, Aisling, was born in 1980 without her right hand, Liam made sure we had regular access to the specialist medical treatment and regular check-ups, despite the logistical difficulties posed by our posting to Africa that year. Amen to you, Liam.

Our open-plan office, all the rage in those days in the civil service, was located on the ground floor of No. 76 St. Stephen's Green, shared with the Department of Justice. A particular hazard of that arrangement was having my desk in close proximity to one colleague whose booming voice on the telephone brought all work to a halt; one could literally not hear oneself think. And as she was deep in the throes of planning for her wedding, the phone calls were quite frequent – and lengthy (and yes, we paid for our private use of the telephone, of course). Ironically, 1974 was the year which saw the long overdue lifting of the marriage ban; imagine, women had to resign from the public service on adopting that status! How far we have come as a society since then, judged not so much by passage of temporal space but in shifting core values, from Conservative to Liberal.

My first boss was a First Secretary and scion of an Ambassador. The officer in question was back from a posting in Berlin. He was a nice man, and infinitely patient though not a great mentor. His reserved manner and frequent absences on health grounds when the pressure of deadlines became intolerable was something we adjusted to as raw Third Secretaries. This was not to be the only time in my career when such scenarios appeared; almost 40 years later, I had to step into a role at short notice to cover for an officer suffering from a mental breakdown at the start of a presidency.

My first Counsellor boss was the redoubtable Pat McCabe, again a lovely guy but a tough cookie, demanding high standards in drafting, a skill I honed through long hours under his supervision.

The role of the After-hours and Weekends Duty Officer has long been a major bone of contention among Third Secretaries, resentful of this imposition from above of extra work for no extra reward, at least not when I had to do it. I believe there is more reward and more consultation these days, even if it still rankles that junior diplomats, like junior doctors, are exploited by the system.

My recurrent nightmare was the embarrassment in front of neighbours of a burly Garda from the Rathmines Station arriving on his motorbike at the shared front door of our modest flat on Wesley Road, Rathgar, helmet under arm, to escort me, or so it seemed, back to the station to relay a message received from Iveagh House that I needed to report in. Usually, it was late on a Friday evening, more often than not requiring replacement at short notice of the proverbial 'lost passport, going on holyers tomorrow'.

Needless to say, the pain of disturbance for such reasons (so-called 'lost' passports often being found after another frantic search of last year's suitcase) was often compensated by forensic interrogation of the client in question and final handing over of the replacement as near as possible to the time of travel. That made some sense at the time.

Sometimes, the call-out was to decode what we then used for secret ticker-tape style messages, known as the 'Dearg' Code (red for danger?). This required tediously slow, Enigma-based calculations of four-letter groups, using a particular 'page of the day' found in a heavy, lead-lined ledger, kept in a humongous safe in the dusty, cobwebbed bowels of Iveagh House to validate the tape spewed out by a machine strongly resembling its infamous Nazi war-time predecessor. And, usually, it was a Head of Mission wondering when he might expect to receive a consignment of Barry's Tea he had ordered via the late-in-arriving diplomatic bag, whereabouts unknown. Such were the joys of a 1970's-era duty officer!

The first Presidency meant long hours and lots of frantic dealings both with other government departments and with our Permanent Mission in Brussels. As a junior officer, I knew next to nothing of the substance and background of the urgent issue in question, but I well remember being caught between a rock and a hard place as my senior Brussels colleagues (addressing me formally by the 'Mr. Denham' moniker to maintain both their dignity and distance in terms of rank and position) pressed, using both copious and lengthy telex and phone calls to demand instructions, usually described in advance, while other Government departments showed a marked irritation at being harried for same and resistant to endorsing the line we sought to pursue.

Ever a system that favours process above results, the arguments between ourselves and the Departments of Industry and Commerce and Finance at senior officials' level were notorious. Round One was a polite enough conversation between myself and a junior equivalent; this quickly escalated to a tussle of Titanic proportions between my boss, he of the spidery handwriting, meticulous in detail but hard to decipher, especially to a lady from the typing pool who was threatening to leave at 5.15 on a Friday no matter what the international crisis, and his opposite number in Industry and Commerce. Not, I should add hastily, that we were implying any mental instability in his character, God forbid, but he defended our traditional exclusive Fyffe's Latin American Banana imports concession to the death in the face of assaults from Caribbean producers who wanted to share the burgeoning EEC market (during Lomé 1 negotiations).

Garrett the Good, as Dr Garret FitzGerald was often called, our distinguished Foreign Minister, was mandated as President to secure this prestigious trade and aid deal with the 64 African, Caribbean & Pacific States (ACP), mostly ex-colonies of France and the UK, during our Presidency. We threw enormous resources into achieving this progressive, unprecedented agreement to be the crowning glory of our First EEC Presidency. Alas, our Industry and Commerce colleague was not impressed, and neither were Finance who didn't want us to incur any significant national share of the inevitable payout to these developing countries as aid in addition to the generous trade concessions. Several rounds of bruising, time-bound, increasingly tendentious exchanges at ever higher levels meant late-night briefing of our then Assistant Secretary in Economic Division; he always tried his best to be patient and to suggest trying a bit harder with our homologues, but it inevitably ended with him picking up the phone to his opposite number and settling the hitherto ferocious arguments in the space of a couple of minutes! I recall that on one occasion our briefing was interrupted by his vivacious wife sweeping into his office unannounced and saying, 'Enough, husband, we need to be leaving for dinner, darling. *Now!*' We had to wait until Monday morning on that occasion for the resolution.

Without exception, Brussels always got their way. Our considerations were always formulaic and rarely influential. This pattern seems to me to have been repeated with relentless monotony over the past 40 years, despite our self-delusional belief that Ireland's voice carries weight in Europe. Unwavering support for the Commission, instigated and insisted upon by Garrett FitzGerald as his enduring legacy to Irish diplomacy, has been the one consistent position we have taken up to recent times.

The six months were gruelling on everyone, none less than on the new recruits. I recall a particularly sad, distressing episode when one of my new colleagues asked to be allowed to leave on time on a particular Friday evening in order to catch the Cork train home. Her request was flatly turned down by our severe old boss who told her, at the end of a flaming shouting match in the corridor, not to bother come back on Monday if she insisted on leaving; she didn't!

The sheer, unabated joy of receiving a brown envelope naming your first posting is one that can never be either matched or repeated. It was preceded by weeks of intense, orgasmic anticipation and speculation; who was going where and how lucky – or not – though in those days few posts apart from Lagos were undesirable for Third Secretaries. Indeed, the true badge of failure was to be informed that one was not being posted; it often was a silence, a lack of envelope that time around that signalled such an ignominious fate. I still maintain that anticipation is 50 per cent of all pleasure!

My own turn came eighteen months into my first job; it was Paris! I couldn't wait to tell Siobhán, who was thrilled, and my parents and sisters, who were slightly more apprehensive!

In those days, we were given no options to negotiate our posting timing. We were given a month's notice (it was mid-March 1976) to up sticks. We didn't need any encouragement! Before the Department could change its mind, we had the tickets issued to us and packers around.

In our excitement to be gone – assisted by leaving behind a very damp flat in Dun Laoghaire that we had been renting, where it rained both inside and out! – we had omitted, for some strange reason I no longer can recall, to pack a canteen of Newbridge cutlery we had been given as a generous wedding present by my work colleagues.

We were also glad to sell on our Renault 4. A shocking, additional £100 garage charge for repairs, including four new tyres, after the original purchase price of £400, had resulted in little improvement in performance. The battery/alternator needed replacing at the same time, but we could never afford to do so, which meant an unseemly morning ritual of 'scooting' the car –

fortunately it was light enough – down the hill from Vesey Place to the main road while jumping in and starting it, hopefully. It usually worked.

The evening return journey was trickier: an elevated office car park with short ramp at the rear of St. Michael's House on Baggot Street, where Siobhán was an early employee of the nascent National Science Council under Dr Liam Downey, did not always work. We were often reliant on – and extremely grateful for – the generosity of passersby, taking pity on the pair of us scooting furiously in rush hour traffic.

By the by, one trick I learnt from Liam Downey, a wily Cork man, as most are, was that if you required a favourable decision on anything, always wait until the afternoon before raising it. Such a strategy has rarely let me down since.

Paris, 1976-79

So it was that we travelled on 26 April 1976 via Aer Lingus 737 from Collinstown to Le Bourget Airport, Paris. En route, Siobhán, comatose as ever on take-off, was mistaken by the air hostess (that's what they were known as in those days) as French; she was delighted! And we sat at the back of the plane so we could smoke!

On arrival, we descended via the rear stairs; a tall, plump silver-haired gent was standing on the tarmac. Before I could say 'Good morning, Ambassador', for it was, indeed, our new lord, His Excellency, a former distinguished Secretary General of the Department, in person. Siobhán says in a loud stage whisper, and rather grumpily as she was left to carry the forgotten cutlery we had taken as hand luggage, 'Who *is* this?' Fortunately, the

Ambassador, who had an entirely justified reputation for enjoying a pretty face, ignored her rudeness!

We travelled from Le Bourget, a famous airport, the first in Paris, long since closed to commercial traffic, in great style in the Official Citroen DS 21, myself in front beside Gianni the driver, Siobhán and his nibs enjoying the comfort of the back.

Gianni was to play a special role in my time as Third Secretary, Consular & Administration, Paris Embassy. As his name would indicate, Gianni was Italian, from near Rome, and drove in a very Roman way, on occasion confusing his sedate DS21 with driving a chariot in the Circus Maximus.

I recall on one occasion being hurtled, sitting in the suicide seat beside him as we conveyed Garrett the Good and an ashen-faced Ambassador to Orly via the Peripherique (similar to the M50) at rush hour on a wintry Friday evening, travelling at warp speed on the hard shoulder for most of the way, and a suicidally inspired weaving in between four lanes of dense, stalled traffic for the remainder.

It was not long after this occasion which, for a junior diplomat, was a normal part of our duties, with no high-risk pay to compensate, that the Ambassador appeared on a Friday evening in my basement office, the equivalent of a rare visit from the Gods to one of their earth-bound minions. I smelled a rat immediately. Sure enough, after the usual flim-flam about what a nice job they had done on the dank bowels of the building, a former royal palace or *hotel particuliere*, and asking how were the monthly accounts coming along, he ventured that he was going to Morocco on the morrow, a secondary accreditation of Ambassador, Paris, and would be away for two weeks (a pleasant yearly obligation). He then requested that the necessary steps be

taken so that Gianni would be gone from his employ by the time
he returned from Fez. I was to ensure the implementation of this
legerdemain wish.

Now, truth be told, Gianni had been in our employ for some
25 years both as Embassy Chauffeur and as Maitre D' during
which time he had been well-known to display his fiery Italian
temper on occasion. He was, therefore, on shaky ground despite
his length of tenure. The real problem was that Gianni, as part of
his conditions of service, inhabited a modest room in the loft and
had no known family or friends. He was, in a word, 'institutionalised' by virtue of his employment.

After a sleepless weekend, I decided that I should follow
the tried and tested civil service precedent of giving Gianni
the bad news on Monday, after lunch. The Ambassador was,
of course, safely away in Morocco at this point in time so I realised I would be the target of Gianni's notorious bad temper. He
spent most of his day wandering around the domestic quarters
with a Gauloise hanging off his lip muttering profanities to himself. Steeling myself to dive under the desk if such drastic evasive
action was called for, I sat Gianni down – his first time ever in my
basement office squat – and rushed out that we thought it was
time he should take a well-earned rest, to retire to his beloved
Italy and could I please have the keys to the official motor and to
his attic abode on my desk by the following Friday?

I need not have worried. He looked at me with his evil eye,
paused until I was quaking uncontrollably, lit another Gauloise
from the one he had begun a short while before and said, '*eh, et
en retour*?' Phew!

A short and perfectly civilised negotiation later, over a glass
of fine chateau red borrowed from the Ambassador's private

stock which Gianni kept on the other side of my basement office wall, we shook hands, hugged, and parted the best of friends. Apparently, Gianni had been angling for some time how to obtain a generous severance package and part of his recent strategy had been to up his seemingly crazy behaviour. His plan was to leave asap for sunnier home climes, somewhere in the south of Italy.

Of course, I never told the Ambassador all that when he returned, tanned and relaxed, and enormously pleased to find Gianni gone. He didn't enquire too deeply as to how I had managed it, but I could tell he held me in some higher esteem, a slightly wondrous glint in his eye whenever the name of Gianni came into our conversation!

Our first-born son, Barry, was conceived in Paris and delivered in the Hôpital de Neuilly, a famous location patronised by the rich and famous who came to Paris and by the foreign Diplomatic Corps who opted for consultations through the medium of English. The McCanns hosted a small celebration after his baptism in the English-speaking parish of St Joseph on Ave. Hoche, where Rose Kennedy was a devout and frequent visitor. It was run by Irish Passionists, hoary types from Belfast for the most part, led by Father Eugene, the most consummate political priest I have ever encountered. He could squeeze funds out of a stone.

But I remember with great sadness that one of the hardest tasks he and I shared was to visit a young Irish student in hospital who had been seriously injured in a road accident. She and her boyfriend had been hitching a lift south to earn some money picking grapes, a popular source of summer fund-raising among Irish undergraduates. The truck they were riding in had been involved in a head-on crash and her boyfriend had been killed. It fell to Eugene and myself to break the news to her and to arrange for her return to Ireland.

Sad episodes such as that were a feature of the cycle of consular incidents that were part of my daily work as Third Secretary.

There was also the drug mule who was caught 'dead to rights, Gov' in possession of a large quantity of heroin as he crossed the Belgian-French border on a train and who ended up in prison near the northern industrial town of Douai, famous for its iron works and the first printed Douai Bible. My task, as I chose to accept it, was to visit the said prisoner and to make sure he was being humanely treated, knew his rights and had legal representation. In order to do so, I had to travel to the far north of France, which I did by train.

The visit itself passed off without too much trauma as 'my convict', *le jeune Irlandais*, seemed to be receiving reasonable treatment in the prison and had not got any major complaints apart from loneliness and language limitations. Of course, under the French Napoleonic Code of law, in contrast to our own Common Law system, he was presumed guilty unless proven otherwise – and there didn't seem much chance of that, given the circumstances of his arrest, caught *in flagrante delicto*, in possession. He seemed happy to see me and to have a chat in our common language. I said I would do so again from time to time, as appropriate.

On my way back, I went into the Douai SNCF station restaurant to while away the time before my train for Paris appeared, not high speed in those days. It was lunch time, so I ordered *entrecote et frites*, followed by *profiteroles*, my all-time favourite, irresistible French dessert. What a delightful culinary discovery did I unearth! Not only were the frites of the best classic French string variety but the hot chocolate sauce that accompanied the profiteroles was served in an elegant, brass doll-size pot which had been made, I discovered, in the local foundry. Only in France and, as I was later to realise, only in SNCF station restaurants, could you find some of the very best of French cuisine, served impeccably and at a reasonable cost. I've kept that a secret for many years since, only telling those I really liked. It explains why seemingly pedestrian SNCF stations all across France always host full dining rooms on a Sunday!

We had many distinguished visitors and other VIPs passing through Paris. Maeve Hillery was a frequent guest of the Ambassador, always on her own and very distant; I never got up the courage to mention that she was present in the Leinster Nursing Home shortly after I was born. Garrett and Joan Fitzgerald, on the other hand, were frequent and friendly Embassy visitors, gentle with each other and with everyone around them, always unfailingly polite and pleasant, great company even for a lowly Third Secretary.

On one occasion, I received an early morning call from the Ambassador to say Gianni was 'under the weather' (this was before the trauma of his Waterloo moment) and would I go quickly to Orly, which had replaced Le Bourget by then as the Aer Lingus Paris destination, to pick up 'Garret & Joan' as they preferred to be known. I was to apologise, which I did profusely, for the unusual carriage, a tiny, early model Peugeot 104, in which they were being taken to the Embassy. Siobhán and myself had only recently purchased it, our very first brand new car.

Peugeots are great to drive, lively and responsive, when they work well. Alas, they are unreliable: we had a litany of poor experiences. Our first 104 blew a plastic oil bung the first day I started it and was off the road for a week. The official 605 in Lusaka had a fuel injection system that seized up the minute you drove on a dirt road. And our sporty 406 in Geneva was like a racehorse: when not galloping, it was in the stable, our local repair shop, most of its life.

To resume, I still then lived in awe of being in their presence, especially Joan who, while extremely nice, could be a trifle intimidating both in presence and in her self-evident intelligence, even when compared with her equally formidable spouse. They made quite a team! What I hadn't calculated that morning, as they came through arrivals, was to see quite such a large amount of luggage in their wake!

Fortunately, the car had four doors, an optional extra version which Siobhán had insisted on buying. We managed, with some difficulty and great ingenuity, not to mention communal discomfort, to get Joan in the rear, together with some smaller pieces of baggage, and Garret in the front, both he and I hunched over the dashboard with our seats as far forward as we could get them to help Joan survive in the back. But I think she did forgive in time, if not forget.

The following Monday, Garret joined the staff for morning coffee, a radical, unheard of gesture and much appreciated by all present; the Ambassador was in somewhat of a huff since Paddy Walsh had arbitrarily moved our coffee venue from his office to a neutral, third floor spare office location. Again, it had been left to me, on the last-in-does-the-dirty-work principle, to inform the Ambassador of this break in tradition. He sulked for weeks before yielding to the inevitable. In those days, coffee in the Counsellor's office had been a leisurely affair, stymieing Paddy from achieving any work from after 11.00 until lunch.

Garret said he had a problem, that he had only just noticed arriving in Paris that his Diplomatic Passport was out of date. Being ever anxious to help, I offered to take it downstairs and stamp it for an extra couple of years; in those days, it was the norm to renew your passport once. Of course, in my haste to oblige, and in my ignorance, as Garret reminded me many years later when we met in San Francisco, I hadn't for a moment appreciated that there was an arcane convention that diplomatic passports should not be renewed. I gather he was embarrassed when this was pointed out to him on his return to Ireland. Nonetheless, it didn't prevent him from asking me, while in San Francisco where I was then Consul General, to sort out a passport issue for one of his grandchildren resident in California. I can only assume that my helpful disposition had also not gone unnoticed!

Before Paris life draws to a close, I would like to record my friendship with colleagues there, Paddy Walsh, Sean Whelan, RIP, Donal Hurley who spent 20 or more years as Agriculture and Trade attaché before being sent off to Teheran to open an Embassy there, Paula Slattery, Joe Brennan and, of course, Angela O'Farrell and the McCanns. Joe and Paula were particularly close friends with whom Siobhán and myself spent a lot of time. Siobhán would occasionally step in to cook for Joe and be in the kitchen when he gave one of his musical soirées. And it is known that the Embassy might occasionally close a few minutes early on a hot summer's afternoon to allow us all to adjourn to a local swimming pool to cool off, always, of course, being available to respond to any emergency that might arise.

That reminds me of the day I offered, in helpful mode again, to accompany a colleague to pick up her new car. It was a Friday afternoon. Paris empties as people head to their country abodes, making the roads in and out of Paris particularly busy, even by Parisian standards. What I hadn't appreciated was that she and I had to travel out to the Ford factory, located to the northeast of the city in a particularly grim industrial suburb. The car was duly produced and handed over after what seemed like endless form-filling. It was a metallic royal blue Ford Escort cabriolet with all the fashionable bells and whistles of the day but that, of course, in 1976, did not extend to any form of navigational aid; hence my role as navigator, or so I thought. She had other plans and ordered me to the driver's side, not one I had ever sat in before!

I successfully resisted this peremptory command (this colleague could use many charms on people, including me, and they usually worked but this time was different). I said that it was her car and that she should be the first to drive it; besides, what would the insurance company say if something happened while I was driving? Fortuitously, she had a momentary aberration, sitting into the left front seat, forgetting that that was the driver's side!

I quickly discovered that my decidedly reluctant colleague had extraordinarily little experience of driving at all, neither right nor left wheel! Negotiating our way through heavy trucks and articulated convoys, we soon reached one of the many bridge crossings of the Seine. I had my head down, engrossed in the map – this was pre-GPS. She said, 'I think I have done something wrong.' I looked up. Sure enough, two of the four wheels of the car had mounted the pavement, crossing the bridge in the wrong direction! No panic, Mr Mannering!

Grabbing the wheel and taking violent evasive action while yelling at her to slam on the brakes, we managed to extricate ourselves and the shiny new car off the bridge footpath and into the right lane. As soon as possible thereafter we swapped places; we drove the rest of the way in silence, parking the car at her request in a space outside the Embassy on Rue Rude. We parted company immediately, me to the corner brasserie for a stiff one or three, my colleague to her apartment where she spent the weekend recovering.

The car stayed in the same place for at least three weeks before she drove it home. There it sat for much of the remaining three years of her time. On the rare occasions I glimpsed it, I would notice a fresh scratch or dint, but nothing was ever said by either of us about that fateful day it first came into her possession.

Of course, a couple of months later, it was my turn to go out to those frightful suburbs and pick up my own new car, our soon-to-be-famous 104. No, I didn't ask her to return the favour!

Siobhán and myself had many happy explorations around France, too many to mention. But I will not quickly forget those made with Liz Ravaud, née Mannion, like myself a product of Greenlea Road, though we didn't know one another at the time. Liz married well, Patrique Ravaud, a banker then working for BNP in Dublin. Patrique was the scion of an extremely wealthy French family whose father ran SNECMA, a French equivalent of Roll Royce or Pratt & Whitney that produced jet aero engines. The father had been an ally of de Gaulle in the resistance.

Liz, a freelance journalist who wrote occasional car review articles, moved back to Paris with Patrique and got herself a French NUJ card. She would often contact Citroen or Peugeot and borrow a car for a weekend which Patrique would drive and Siobhán and myself would happily sit in the back. On one occasion we drove to Cahors and Liz arranged an old farmhouse for us to rent. The bedroom arrangements were, I recall, quite intimate with exceedingly thin walls between us in the loft. Liz was not shy when providing a running commentary on her bed-time pursuits! And every consensus decision made that weekend was preceded by Liz saying, 'This is my car and we will go…' or 'This is my house and we will eat…' Steak for breakfast was a rare treat for us all. We had fun – and copious tastings of the wonderful local wine!

France is a patchwork quilt of different cultures, culinary de-lights and wines to tickle the palate. But our time there reluctant-ly came to an end as we packed up for our African safari. It had been an almost four-year *Lune de Miel*!

Chapter 2

Lusaka or Osaka?

Homeless in Dublin; African adventures; coup or cu? Father Michael, cannabis expert; Tom Murphy's Limericks; called to State House after wild party; weather forecasts; Maeve Binchy's loo break

Having decided that we were quite happy to live in relative poverty in Paris for the rest of our lives (the French don't really have any concept of social poverty, being the spoilt children of Europe, *les enfants gat*ées, since 1957), along pops future Secretary General Dermot Gallagher to the Embassy basement where Consular had been newly housed, to meet me. Ostensibly attending an OECD meeting in their fancy Chateau de la Muette, I didn't know it then, but he was checking out my performance.

At that time, in mid-1979, Dermot was in charge of our nascent Irish aid programme, then unimaginatively called Development Cooperation Division. I always felt *Eiraid* would have been catchier but don't mention the war. The aid programme was itself expanding rapidly under Dr Garret Fitzgerald and promotions were happening all around me; my old friend and former Private Secretary to Charles Haughey, Martin Green, had opened an aid office in Lesotho the previous year, passing through Paris en route.

So, several weeks after Dermot's visit, I received a brown envelope with a letter offering me a much sought-after promotion from Third to First Secretary; remember, there were 30 of us who had eagerly joined the Irish diplomatic service in 1974 so promotions were like gold dust. Already, a whiff of competitive behaviour was seeping through the old high walls of Iveagh House as a new breed of mandarin began to displace the old guard. Dr. G.F. was nothing if not progressive.

However, there was a catch. I had to go to Lusaka, Zambia, central Africa, to activate the offer. Martin Green had warned that this was the strategy being adopted by HQ; offer a promotion but link it to filling a challenging post. This pattern was to be repeated many times over as our empire expanded into more exotic parts. It became routine when trying to find a volunteer for places like Lagos.

So, of course, after a moment's hesitation to check a dusty world atlas, there being no Google in those days, a brief plea to Siobhán to trust me, and the thrill of telling my parents of my promotion, followed, *sotto voce*, by the word Lusaka, I agreed. HQ were delighted (as was Dermot, who now had filled both new aid posts, Lusaka and Dar-es-Salaam, which Brendan Scannell had opted for on first refusal); my parents less so. It wasn't until many years later that I understood the full pain of seeing a child and grandchildren so far away and so remote.

Siobhán was carrying our second child; Barry, our first, was then 10 months old when we packed up our year-old Ford Cortina (left-hand drive as we always expected to be moving on to a foreign destination after Paris if we had to leave it) and drove home via the relatively new Irish Ferries crossing from Le Havre to Rosslare. I always remember it was a glorious, sunny day along the Seine and our sadness at leaving was bittersweet, indeed, tempered by thoughts of an African adventure.

With no immediate home in Dublin to which to return, Pat, my former boss at HQ, and Patricia O'Connor, his elegant spouse, kindly, rashly, offered to put us up in their spare room in their home in Killiney. I am sure they didn't anticipate weeks turning into months but they never conveyed any limit to their generous hospitality.

In a rare moment of logic, I had been offered a recce visit to Lusaka to see it for myself, via a visit to Maseru to be briefed by Martin on what a 'Development Cooperation Officer' was supposed to do. This was very much an on-the-job learning experience at work. I accepted with alacrity, needing to know, with Siobhán now pregnant again, what maternity services were like locally.

A slight delay was occasioned by receipt of an air ticket, destination Osaka and return. For one brief moment, the thought occurred I could go there and no one would likely know the difference.

Dream over, I flew out to spend a few days, firstly to meet my new Ambassador in Nairobi, H.E. Michael Green. Officially, I was one of his staff, as was the other new boy on the block, my good friend Brendan Scannell, recently arrived in Dar es Salaam. Michael was a good Clare man, known in the Department for his exuberant character. Alas, ill health was to dog him later on and he passed away relatively young.

Despite the beauty of Nairobi, then a bustling, seemingly prosperous African capital, I was happy enough to leave again for Lesotho to spend a further week en route to Lusaka, with the Ambassador's namesake, but no relation, Martin Green, 'Our Man' in Maseru.

Regional relationships were tense. There were no diplomatic relations between Zambia and South Africa (RSA) at the time, so no direct flights either. A war was simmering between Namibian freedom fighters and South Africa, and the putative government of Namibia was housed in the UN Institute of Namibia in Lusaka; more of which anon. Southern Rhodesia was on the cusp of independence. Lesotho is surrounded by RSA so the only way in was to fly to Johannesburg and on to Maseru. I wasn't impressed by Jo'burg; a smouldering atmosphere, smoke clouding over the horizon from surrounding massive townships. I stayed close to my airport Holiday Inn hotel for the overnight.

Maseru was a revelation; friendly locals, smart centre, decent offices and hotel, golf courses, modern architecture, verdant countryside and the all-pervasive Maseru Country Club! Life seemed to revolve, at least for the expatriates, around the Country Club. It was there I first heard the frightening tales of life on the edge in Zambia. The look of horror and consternation that greeted my naive revelation of my destination, Lusaka, and not just for a visit but for the foreseeable future! No one I met in Maseru had anything positive to say about that wild frontier country to the far north! But then, as I subsequently discovered, none of my spooky interlocutors had ever been there!

Visits to various aid projects already underway, including the high impact, stunningly visual Pony Project deep in the high mountains near the source of the Orange River – shades of Tolkien! – restored my confidence somewhat. Apart, that is, from the hairy ride in the official Toyota Landcruiser, Martin pressed over the steering wheel, four-wheel drive engaged, alongside steep gorges over non-existent tracks, bumped by rock and sliding along streams as we edged up the mountain to the pony paddocks at its peak. Sometime later, I heard that Martin had written off the Landcruiser on a subsequent journey, thankfully with little damage to himself. It was the first of several challenging driving experiences for him and a portent of what I was to face myself in Lusaka a few months later.

Forewarned by those I had spoken with in Maseru not to expect anything good from where I was going, and with a sense of foreboding that increased as we took off from Maseru bound for Malawi, the meeting point of SAA with a Zambia Airways connection to Lusaka, I fell in with the company of a lovely Irish nurse while waiting in the airport in Lilongwe. She was on her way back to the Zambia Copperbelt and she reassured me that life in Zambia was not something to fear, despite the tall tales I had been filled with in Maseru.

Our Zambia Airways 737 tilted her nose to the sun as we roared down the short runway and a distinctive lyrical accent, oh so familiar, told us to sit back and relax on our short hop to Lusaka. As I discovered later, Aer Lingus had just been awarded a turn-key contract to manage and operate the airline. Aer Lingus had a team of pilots, engineers and managers (about 50 in all) on the ground and many of them became firm friends over the years.

My initial impression of Zambia was of a remote, flat country, filled with deep purple Jacaranda trees and masses of Bougainvillea of all shades, flame trees and avocado bushes, a rich and slightly mysterious and romantic landscape.

My host was Conor McIntyre, a man in his mid-sixties who had been our Honorary Consul for several decades, having come to settle in what was then the Federation of Northern Rhodesia and Nyasaland (Malawi). Conor was a veritable 'rough diamond' who had left County Mayo at the age of 14 and headed to Manchester with little in the way of formal education and less money, but with a a natural talent as an entrepreneur. A self-taught truck driver, he soon became a truck owner. As the Great Depression gave way to war preparations, Conor began to buy a fleet of trucks which made him a fortune during World War II. Armed with a sense of adventure, the bold Conor headed to central Africa where he quickly established a building materials empire with, for example, a monopoly on local brick-making.

Zambia was beginning to emerge, post-war, as a major source of copper at a time when telephonic communications were growing exponentially on the back of copper wire. Conor made it his business to supply the northern Copperbelt mining region of the country with all it needed from the construction industry. He never looked back.

By the time I arrived in Lusaka in 1980, Conor was ensconced in a mansion in the exclusive Kabalonga, Leopard's Hill district on the outskirts of Lusaka, close to the President's State House official residence, later the site of my near-death experience. He also had an extensive portfolio of housing stock, one of which he would make available to rent to the Irish Government for my use; an offer we both came to regret accepting.

Conor hadn't endeared himself on first acquaintance; in fact, our first encounter didn't happen! Admittedly, telephonic communications with Zambia in those days were sporadic and challenging. Telephone calls had to be booked days in advance. Telex machines were still few and far between; telegrams were still in use: Long live Wells Fargo and Western Union! Conor had a telephone but never answered it. Our telegrams advising him of my arrival had gone unanswered so I wasn't entirely surprised to find he wasn't at the airport on arrival. A taxi got me to 'the Intercon' (Intercontinental Hotel) as it was known. It took me two days to track Conor down; he claimed at the time he had been in the Copperbelt and hadn't got the message, but I quickly realised in subsequent conversations that Conor was a man of strong views, that being replaced by what he saw as an upstart diplomat wasn't high on his priority list and that he had mixed feelings about Ireland and what it had done for him!

Having the Honorary Consul status was a useful business tool, but Conor had few friends among the 'expats'. He did, however, have an interesting relationship with the local, native Zambian population. On one occasion, he introduced me to a close advisor of President Kenneth Kaunda and, as we were walking away, said in a loud stage whisper, 'He was a tea boy in my office, don't ya know!'

What I did find out in that exploratory week visit was that local maternity facilities were basic and definitely not to be risked; the expat population decamped to South Africa for all but routine medical treatment. Even basic medicines were in short supply; it helped to have missionary connections.

So I went home to Dublin a little sadder and a lot wiser. In those times, 'The Department' had an almost human personality, an abundance of compassion and much less regulation – that ratio has since reversed to a significant extent but such is progress. Our decent Head of Personnel for many years, Liam Rigney, understood our concerns and it was decided I could wait and work in Development Aid at HQ until our second child was born.

Which was just as well as she arrived with only her left hand which came as a shock both to her parents and to her delivery team in Holles Street, as you may imagine. However, the gruff but kindly specialist in artificial limbs at the National Rehab Hospital on Rochestown Avenue, a man of few but wise words, assured us that all would be well. He counselled that we should treat Aisling as we would any two-handed child and that she would learn to do everything that a two-handed person could do.

And his prediction was entirely accurate, as Aisling subsequently proved to everyone she met. Her prowess on the hockey pitch for Loreto Dalkey was an early indication of what was to follow; her mountain biking and skiing in the French Alps became the stuff of family legend; and her insistence of passing her driving test, first time, without any artificial aids, made Irish driving test history! Not to mention her full academic achievements which includes going on to achieve an M.Sc. in Forensic Science.

Meanwhile, even the generosity of our hosts was wearing thin so we rented a house in Churchtown. Shortly thereafter, as a supernumerary, I was despatched at a day's notice to mind the Embassy in Stockholm while the Ambassador there, Dermot Waldron, flew to Poland, his secondary accreditation, to arrange for a coal supply for what then was still a high dependency Irish market dominated by a small number of suppliers. This situation had arisen because our normal source, the coal mines of West Virginia, had shut down due to a lightning miners' strike, denying our local companies their usual supply. Poland was then a tightly State-controlled communist regime so Waldron had his work cut out. So much for diplomats not getting their hands dirty! Anyway, to my advantage, it took him three weeks to complete negotiations.

The reason I was sent was that the Third Secretary of the Embassy in Stockholm was at HQ handling important Lomé II negotiations between the EEC and 46 African, Caribbean and Pacific nations (the ACP). I was given no time to mention to the Personnel Officer who had approached me with the last-minute request to replace my missing Stockholm colleague that I had been a raw Third Sec at HQ in 1975 when Lomé I was being negotiated. That is my story and I am sticking to it!

Three idyllic weeks in Stockholm were interrupted by a hysterical phone call from Siobhán to say the house in Churchtown had been burgled early on Saturday morning. Fortunately, both Siobhán and our baby son were unharmed and the burglar had left after helping himself to a glass of milk and biscuit in the kitchen!

We eventually got going to Lusaka on 16 April, 1980, arriving at Lusaka International with an eighteen month and a six-week-old baby in tow. As the plane circled to land, I noticed a large crowd on the runway and a band and military parade in progress. I turned to Siobhán and said, 'I think Conor is trying to make up for the last time I arrived here!' In fact, it was the pre-departure ceremony for President Kaunda who was on his way south to Harare, then Salisbury, to celebrate the Independence of Zimbabwe, then Southern Rhodesia, at midnight that day. I felt it was a good omen!

Does anyone remember the grainy black and white ITV programme, *On Safari, with Armand and Mikaela Denis?* It was from a mid-1950s, white perspective, only a pale reflection of the reality of life in the African bush. Zambia is blessed with excellent wild life reserves and with an aid programme spread over a country the size of France and Germany combined, with a population of only 8 million in 1980 (now 18 million). I had many opportunities to see it first-hand.

But I will not soon forget the day I took Frank Cogan, a good friend and perfect gentleman, married to a wonderful woman, Pauline, out in our Peugeot to the remote Okavango reserve bordering the Caprivi Strip. Frank was then in charge of Development Aid at HQ, and on his first aid inspection visit to Africa. At the time, I was more concerned about getting too close to rebel activity in this area bordering Zambia and Namibia than to the local fauna.

But nothing prepared us for emerging onto a plain right in the middle of a large herd of grazing elephants. As we drew ever nearer, with Frank happily snapping away on his camera beside me, I began to notice that a number of the elephants were looking in our direction and a lot of ear-flapping was going on. The next minute, they started to trundle quite quickly towards the car. Exercising the best three-point turn, and the quickest, I had ever attempted, we managed to evade the now madly charging beasts by a whisker. Close up elephant-watching is not recommended for pregnant mothers or those with a heart condition! I learnt later that ear-flapping is a warning sign by the females when protecting younger animals. The saying 'an elephant at the table' has never been the same since! By the way, I don't think I told Frank at the time but the car, a 605, had an ugly reputation for stalling with clogged fuel jets when driven on unpaved roads.

Kenneth Kaunda was President of Zambia, leading the country to independence from Britain in 1964. 'KK', as he was affectionately known, was a great admirer of Irish independence and the role model of de Valera (Michael Collins was not well-known in those pre-movie days). This sense of solidarity with African independence movements was, of course, a reputation we enjoyed as a former British colony ourselves before our sovereign foreign policy was subsumed by that of the mighty European Union with its significant number of former imperial powers. Happily, this phenomenon goes largely unnoticed during our Security Council election campaigns.

KK's first visit to Europe after that date was to Ireland, even before the UK, in order to recruit judges, medical practitioners (a notable example being Jackie Kyle), teachers and other administrators to support his country's struggle with the daunting legacy of colonialism. I was struck to hear that at independence in 1964, Zambia had a wonderful infrastructure of roads and public buildings left by its colonial master, but that only 3 per cent of the population had received any formal education at all, and that only 3 per cent of that group went beyond primary schooling. What a challenge Africa faced as empires retreated! Harold Macmillan's famous 'Winds of Change' speech in Cape Town in 1960 took on real meaning.

Apart from his famous, large white handkerchief, always carried between the fingers of his right hand, Kenneth Kaunda had a famous slogan, 'One Zambia! One Nation!' Local wags added rather unkindly, 'One Zambia, one nation, one railway, one station!' or, even more cruelly, 'One Zambia, one nation, one telly, one station!'

I recall early on watching a Special Broadcast by Zambia Television which featured KK in the TV studio in Lusaka and his Prime Minister of the time, Humphrey Mulemba, who was inaugurating a live video link from a new studio in Chipata, the

Eastern Province regional capital, about 1,000 kilometres away on the Malawi border.

Humphrey picks up a telephone and shouts down into it, 'Isn't this great modern technology, Mr. President?!'

President Kaunda, eyes alight and a big grin on his face, waved his signature handkerchief at the screen and said, 'No, Humphrey, it is magic, Humphrey, MAGIC!' Such was the arrival of late twentieth century technological development!

And, of course, there were the elegant, remarkable Zambian Army Officer Cadets who were sent, not to Sandhurst, but to the Curragh of Kildare to complete their training. Indeed, I recall seeing them strolling along O'Connell Street in their smart khaki green uniforms, resplendent with brilliant white cross-belts. Little did I know then that I would end up being the first Irish diplomat to take up residence in Zambia some 15 years later in a country whose Defence Forces Officer Corps had been trained on the Curragh of Kildare. Alas, at least one of them had higher ambitions.

About six months into our posting, and still living in – and working from – the Pamodzi Hotel, while waiting patiently and naively for Conor's promise of a house to materialise, the nightly news on Zambia Television came on air with a dramatic breaking story of an attempted coup led by a disaffected army officer in the Western Province. The coup was quickly put down by a nervous regime but not before we enjoyed six weeks of curfew from 6.00 pm to 6.00 am.

I say enjoyed because it was a unique time of all-night stay-over parties, enlivened by a fashion for endless games of Yahtzee and lots of good conversation. During one of these, with a British accountant, I discovered that it was his house, one of the many owned by our Hon. Consul, which he had generously offered to us as a permanent residence once the sitting tenants left. Alas, no one had bothered to tell my new friend the accountant, who quickly disabused me of any intention on his part to leave the property.

A frantic search for Conor the following day tracked him down to his office at the brick works. Conor was not amused to hear of my encounter the night before with his tenant. Blustering that he had given notice of his intention to take back the house (he had even taken us on a visit to measure for curtains while the tenant was on long leave in the UK), Conor told me to leave it with him and he would set the matter to rights.

Next I read in the local newspaper, the *Zambia Daily Mail*, reporting (no story was ever too small to report) that a well-known local businessman, Conor McIntyre, had been the subject of a Court Restraint Order preventing him from setting foot on his property at a certain location in the suburb of Kabalonga. The reason given was that McIntyre had visited the property without the tenant's knowledge or consent while the tenant was at work the previous day, and had removed both the front gate and the house's front door! It wasn't long before friends began asking me if this was the same house Conor had promised to the Irish government for our use. Needless to say, our six months of patiently waiting to take possession, 'plámásed' by various credible excuses from Conor along the way, was at an end.

Furious with him, and at the end of my proverbial tether, I stormed off to the one and only furniture store in Lusaka to cancel all the furniture items we had reserved prior to moving in. As luck would have it, or more likely an answer to the prayers of some of the 400 or so Irish missionaries in Zambia that I had enlisted in the cause, the shop manager, obviously devastated at the prospect of losing one of the biggest orders of his life, recalled that a customer had just been in to order kitchen furniture for a new house he had just built for himself. This, I well recall, was at the end of the day on a Friday. A phone call later, I had an appointment to visit early Saturday morning. The rest is now history as they say.

No. 6663 Katima Mulilo Road, also known as Steam Engine Road, was not in the fancy neighbourhood of Kabalonga we had been promised; rather, it was in the new suburb of Roma on the unfashionable side of the city. But the local Reuters correspondent had his house and office down the road, and the Irish Franciscan Sisters, the Irish Sisters of Charity, the Irish Jesuits and the Kiltegans all had houses nearby so at least we had some interesting neighbours. We also had a small but perfectly formed pool and a tennis court-cum-open-air reception space and, most importantly, a vegetable garden and a two-room guest cottage at the end of the garden with a separate entrance, which allowed me to boast that I walked to and from work, twice a day, every day (and had a swim after lunch and after work).

A short but sweet negotiation later, two logistics and accommodation problems were solved in one fell swoop – and just in time, as it turned out. Three weeks later, the Aussies arrived in town, looking for accommodation for a new High Commission to open in Zambia. While we ended up firm friends, H.E. Michael Potts and crew were obliged to wait nearly two years before finding a permanent residence. He often rued the day they had arrived three weeks' late for No. 6663!

I recall we were the fortunate recipients early on of the encyclopaedic knowledge of Father Michael Kelly SJ (called the elder

Michael to distinguish him from his younger namesake, also a Jesuit, also in Lusaka), whose favourite pastime was tending his remarkable array of fruit and vegetable species in their retreat house back garden, a vast plot of several acres he had carved out of the bush over a number of years. At 6663, we employed a young man by the name of Joseph to tend our own modest vegetable patch (later torn up, I heard, by one of my successors to provide space for a new, large office for the Ambassador, alas) under Michael's close supervision.

On one such inspection visit, Michael called my attention to a lovely, yellow-flowering shrub next to the much-anticipated asparagus crop in the making (one of the many blessings of that part of Africa is that you could stick anything in the ground and it would grow and thrive!). The flowering plant in question, I was told, was local cannabis which Joseph had planted for his own recreational use. It goes without saying that the plant ended up on our rapidly growing compost heap while Joseph explored other career opportunities!

Michael, who was Vice Rector of the University of Zambia, went on to become a renowned expert on education in Africa, frequently consulted for his advice by The World Bank. He visited us there in 1988, describing his impression of the United States on first acquaintance as 'a desperately obedient society'. Michael was also centrally involved in fighting the spread of Aids as it took hold among African society. Many years later, in 2012, Michael was among the initial group of recipients of the President's Distinguished Service Award for Irish Abroad, and in 2020 was honoured with the issue of a commemorative stamp in the Irish Abroad series. He thoroughly deserved both national honours!

We soon began to have lots of visits from Ireland as word spread that Ireland had opened a resident presence in Lusaka. I recall that in our second year there we counted some 54 inward visits in 52 weeks; quite a logistical feat. The Institute of Public Administration, of course, under the able leadership of Colm O'Nualain and Joan Corkery, had long-established links with their equivalent body in Lusaka, NIPA. Indeed, we can boast that just as the Zambian army had been trained by ours, so the senior management of the Zambian civil service had honed their skills in Lansdowne Road! Other Irish entities exploring links with Zambia included the IDA, IDI, EI, BFE and not least, HEDCO, the third-level umbrella body under Paud Murphy, the cousin of a colleague, Padraig Murphy. Paud later secured a position in The World Bank. Among the many other visitors too numerous to mention were Jim Flanagan from the Department of Agriculture who supervised the Dairy Farm project. Jim, an extremely engaging and knowledgeable companion, was famous for walking the length and breadth of the two farms on his regular visits, usually stripped down to his string vest and good suit trousers and court shoes! He, too, went on to greater things.

One of our most memorable visitors was Dr Tom Murphy, President of UCD at the time. Tom, who stayed with Siobhán and myself during his visit, regaled us over breakfast, lunch and dinner with his talent for composing impromptu limericks. I recall he also told us that when he had addressed the La Leche League a few years previously, he had started his speech by saying, 'Ladies, the first time I had a tit in my mouth was when I was a second-year medical student!' The ladies were not amused, needless to say, but Tom chortled away merrily!

He was accompanied on that trip by eminent Professor of Development Economics and close friend Dr Helen O'Neill and by Paud Murphy. We travelled up to Ndola on the Copperbelt to visit the nascent University of Zambia campus there. That night, we all stayed at the only hotel in town and had our inevitable chicken and rice meal together.

Tom, then just 65 and never a man to sit still despite, or perhaps because of, his new pacemaker, took to the hotel's dance floor and danced the night away with several lovely lasses from the locality. Finally, at 2.00 am, the dancing stopped and Tom returned to our table where the rest of us had engaged in desultory conversation while waiting for Tom to retire. I asked him how he did it, where he got the tremendous energy from to keep up with his dance companions? His reply was succinct and instructive: 'Donal,' he said patiently, with a smile always on his pleasant face, ' Donal, young man, it's like this … at my age, you are flattered when they say "Yes" … and relieved when they say "No!"'

Shortly after my arrival in Lusaka, I was to come off worse myself from a close encounter with an army truck turning right on to the main road leading past State House one Saturday afternoon. No stopping, not even slowing down, the truck emerged from the front gates, barrelled across the central reservation and appeared in front of me in the time it takes to type this sentence. I swerved to avoid being sideswiped but in that process, hit the kerb, broke the steering rods and came to a stop while gently rolling over once. I was relatively unscathed as my speed was low enough and I clambered out, shaken but not stirred, to see the army lorry disappear in a cloud of dust. A diplomatic protest to the Ministry elicited an apology but no compensation for the damaged vehicle or its unfortunate driver.

Life was lived on the edge and to the full in Zambia, in technicolour with both the beauty and brutality of a society in rapid transition. A particularly sad case was that of Joe Fanning, a childhood friend from Rathgar whom I met again for the first time in 1982 in Lusaka; Joe had, in the meantime, become a senior Director in Anglo-American Mining Corporation, the dominant private sector partner with the Government in the state's copper mines. By coincidence, Joe's first cousin, Frank Taylor, is a Kiltegan missionary, first in Zambia, then in Malawi. Frank had himself survived an ambush at one of the mission stations.

Eight months after leaving Zambia (Joe was, I recall, among a large group of friends who bid us a tearful farewell from Lusaka International in 1983, this time without any presidential fanfare to distract from it!) I received a traumatic phone call from a mutual friend in Zambia to say that Joe had been shot dead earlier that day while picking up his son from school on their way to the airport to pick up their daughter returning for the summer holidays from boarding school in Europe. Again, I was dumbfounded by this literally shocking news. The perpetrators had shot him while driving away in Joe's car, having taken his wallet and keys at gunpoint in front of all the other parents picking up their children.

On a somewhat happier note, and going back to shortly after the post-coup curfew, one dinner party we hosted for departing Aer Lingus engineer Frank O'Rourke and his delightful spouse Kay (and loving mother of a beautiful family) went exceptionally late; it was after 3.00 am and too many empty bottles later that the last guest departed after the usual nostalgic sing-song; the neighbours never complained.

Imagine my fright when the phone rang three hours later at 6.00 am and a stern voice boomed down the line to my groggy state, 'This is State House! The President wants to see you!' My first reaction was bum-squeezing terror; my second was to suspect a practical joker, of which there were a few around town. A quick return phone call ascertained that it was, indeed, State House, and that I was, indeed, being summoned to appear later in the day! No further explanation was forthcoming.

Why was I being summoned? Had the neighbours reported my calls of a coup during the early hours? Our landlord, later brother-in-law, Brian, had given us a puppy from the litter of Pyrenean mountain dogs he bred. Big and white, his aggressive father was named Caesar. It didn't take long to call ours Cuchulain. But that quickly became shortened to 'Cu', and so I shouted early that Saturday morning after the party for Cu who had an inclination to wander around our property at night. It was only later on that it occurred to me that I might have been calling out 'Cu! Cu!' a bit too loudly, considering what had occurred a short time ago. Or had someone reported the raucous conversations that some of our guests had engaged in, not always flattering to the local society?

Fortunately for me, the truth was more mundane and I did not have to tell HQ I was being made 'PNG' (Persona Non Grata, the worst fate that can befall a resident diplomat) for treasonable behaviour. The president, who was an utterly charming, gentle man, and who was far better informed about the Irish aid programme than I ever could have thought, had decided that he wanted to send two of his twelve children, adopted twins, to college in Ireland at his own expense. I was both greatly relieved and very happy to facilitate his request.

President Kaunda was one of the first of his initial post-colonial generation of African leaders to bow to the will of the Zambian electorate and surrender power through a peaceful and orderly transition to his Independence Party's opposition when they won the 1990 election. While he was not particularly well-treated in retirement, it was with great personal sadness that I learnt of President Kaunda's passing at the great age of 97 in June 2021.

Zambia was also the place where I learned of the hierarchy of diplomatic office, jealously guarded by elderly diplomats who zealously preached and practiced the tenet of 'learning to grow into privilege'.

One such manifestation of this was to occur early on in meetings of the local Heads of Mission of what were then the nine Member States of the European Community. Greece joined in 1981 and was represented in Lusaka by a long-time Honorary Consul and owner of what was the only supermarket in town. He was not shy about exercising power over the distribution of scarce products, for example, butter, which appeared only rarely and never on the shelves, but that is a story for another occasion.

Coordination among the Member States was at an elementary stage, confined to monthly lunches by whoever held the EC six-month rotating Presidency, preceded by earnest informal group conversation during which each colleague would attempt to show they had better gossip than the other about what our hosts were up to, usually no good in their opinion.

I remember the first lunch of the 1983 French Presidency, hosted by the distinguished Ambassadeur de France whose first name was Jacques. Directly opposite Jacques at his long and immaculately laid table sat the British High Commissioner, Sir

Johnny, a tall and elegant gent but with a rather remote, haughty manner which was quite intimidating, especially to a relatively junior officer like me. Sir Johnny liked to play up his special status as a High Commissioner in a Commonwealth country.

For some strange reason relating to the rotating Presidency and my time en poste, I had ended up sitting to Sir Johnny's right, a location he chose largely to ignore for much of the lunch, focusing his attention instead across the table from our host.

Johnny to Jacques: 'Jacques, mon ami, this red wine you are serving us today is rather fine. Did you have it shipped directly from la belle France?'

Jacques to Johnny: 'Mais oui, Sir Johnny; I had it flown in on the UTA flight earlier this week, especially for our lunch today' (UTA was the then airline of France serving the African continent).

Pregnant pause.

High Commissioner to Irish colleague, drawing himself up to his full height while seated and looking directly down his nose: 'I suppose, Mr Denham (thereby emphasising the gulf in our status), that like me, you depend on the local supply, severely limited in choice, of wine from South Africa?'

Me to Sir Johnny (seeing a chance to put one over on the auld enemy): 'Actually, Sir Johnny, I recently shared in a delivery of Australian wine imported by our colleague, the Australian High Commissioner', delivered with a broad smile.

Pregnant pause once more.

High Commissioner to Irish colleague, looking down his long, aquiline nose again at me, returning my smile this time with a glint of checkmate in his eyes: 'Aaah, yes, indeed . . . another fine colonial wine!' Turns away; end of conversation.

In fact, the status of our office in Zambia was unorthodox. Formally, Department of Foreign Affairs (DFA) was obliged to comply with Department of Finance restrictions in force at the time, which precluded the opening of any new Irish diplomatic missions. The DFA was determined not to be outdone by the mean-minded approach of our Finance equivalents who, by the way, jealously guarded for themselves a higher grade payment system for many years to underline their superiority, something that rankled with their opposite numbers in all other departments.

In one of many examples of ingenuity still extant today, the Department came up with the formula of 'an aid office of the Embassy of Ireland to Kenya' to describe the resident diplomats it had placed in Dar-es-Salaam (my good friend, Brendan Scannell) and in Lusaka (mise).

Finance didn't blink, though the huge amount Michael Greene boasted he had paid for his palatial residence in Nairobi a year earlier in 1979, as a period of austerity at home began to bite, stuck in that Department's craw. Fast forward to the next austerity era in 1987-8 and, with malice aforethought, Finance claim the scalp of Embassy Nairobi, closing that mission down and selling off the residence for short-term gain. Fortunately, it is now reopened, though the damage done by closure is still evident when talking to proud Kenyans.

But, back to Lusaka in 1980, the local Foreign Ministry, whose Protocol Department was one of the strongest within it and a stickler for diplomatic precedent, refused to recognise our 'special status' or lack thereof. So I was faced with allowing them to put a more conventional format of 'Charge d'Affaires' on my diplomatic ID card and of adopting Embassy of Ireland in large letters with aid office in finer print. This also only lasted for a relatively short period as the *de facto* eventually also became *de jure*.

One of my more curious experiences as an Aid official vis-à-vis the European Community (now EU) in Zambia was when I suggested, in 1981, not long after I had settled in to my posting, that the EC aid attachés might meet together to exchange information on what we were each individually doing on the ground in Zambia; I did so out of curiosity but with little expectation of what it would throw up.

The idea was seized upon with alacrity by my Dutch colleague who agreed to host the meeting at his office in their purpose-built embassy; in those days, the Dutch could be counted upon, like ourselves, to be enthusiastic Europeans and advocates of close cooperation as such. Unlike my laconic British colleague who, even back then, exhibited indifference bordering on detachment. How times have changed! The EC was represented in Zambia by a former senior colleague, Hugh Swift, as ever perceptive, intelligent and committed; we protected each other's back. Hugh's spouse, Maura, had successfully applied herself to learning one of the main local languages, a feat almost without precedent among the expat community, apart from our missionary friends. So, the afternoon came for our meeting.

We began, as per precedent, by a 'tour de table', with each colleague in turn describing what projects they were engaged upon in Zambia. So, the Danes talked about their wheat project, the Germans about their clean water development project, the EU about its financial support project in the Ministry of Finance and so on. I mentioned our dairy farm project, our water well project, our teacher support project at third level and our cement factory project. Each secretly felt rather self-satisfied and quietly confident, in a spirit of friendly competitiveness, that they had chosen the best and most innovative projects to support.

Well, imagine our surprise and dismay as it became crystal clear that the Government of Zambia, whom we all had naively assumed to be a passive, compliant, do-as-you-wish partner in our aid endeavours, turned out to have been a wily, even devious, co-conspirator, controlling adroitly exactly what went on in the aid field in Zambia by welcoming everyone's offers to help but then directing donors to their 'most urgent needs'. We had collectively and individually truly had the wool pulled over our eyes!

What we had seen as ground-breaking Irish Aid projects had been tried and failed by other donors in the past, and vice-versa, and no one had been informed of this sealed loop of assistance. It meant, of course, that Zambia had adopted an almost zombie-like approach to aid, furnishing their list of never-changing priorities and perpetuating a relatively small pool of projects ad infinitum, or so they had thought.

Needless to say, none of us was best pleased to discover this deception and the quite valuable lesson learnt was to adopt a rather harder analytical approach before taking on any new project suggested by those in authority. It also spelled a sea-change to the type of aid project undertaken, with less direct intervention (for example, running dairy farms or cement factories) and far more local community involvement. Fortunately, we never gave any direct funding into Zambian Government coffers so we were not threatened by abuse of funds such as happened much later in Uganda; that was, sadly, one lesson seemingly not well learnt in that case.

In Zambia and elsewhere in the 1980s there was a relatively simple approach to dispensing aid financing and hands-on aid management; nostalgia is a toxic indulgence, but I cannot help but wonder if simpler wasn't also more effective?

One particular Irish aid project I am particularly proud of was the Suburban Maternity Clinics project, an inspiration of Dr Mona Tyndall. Mona, a Holy Rosary sister from Killeshandra, County Cavan, and a gynaecologist of excellent reputation in Lusaka, visited my office one day in 1982 and asked if I would like to visit Lusaka General Hospital, known as the University Teaching Hospital (UTH), formerly a maternity hospital in pre-independence days and designed to deliver some 5,000 babies a year when it opened in the late 1950s. UTH had seen better days; what I discovered on accompanying Mona on one of her rounds was a scene worthy of any Irish A&E, with women giving birth out in the corridors on emergency trollies, some 25,000 of them in 1981. Mona said little but the scene I witnessed that day spoke for itself.

Mona's proposal to me to alleviate this unsustainable situation was, like the woman herself, practical and direct in its approach: to provide training for midwives who would staff a series of suburban health clinics in the townships which ringed Lusaka, many of them recently built by World Bank funding but lying idle owing to operational resource and staff constraints.

To overcome the reluctance of the maternal population to go to the clinic to give birth rather than travelling all the way in to UTH, and to provide psychological encouragement to mothers-to-be to use these clinics, a small fleet of reconditioned ambulances would be fitted out with a mobile radio link (remember, this was in an era well before mobile phones) which would allow them to respond quickly to any emergency birth complications and whisk the patient into UTH. A solution elegant in its simplicity.

Convincing my colleagues at HQ to support this project through funding for the recruitment and training of midwives under Mona's direct supervision, plus funds to recondition ambulances and to provide radio receivers, was not difficult and agreement came relatively quickly. But what neither Mona nor myself anticipated was the initial reaction of the UK-educated Permanent Secretary of the Ministry of Health, himself a trained surgeon, which was to insist on a fleet of brand-new ambulances, preferably German-sourced.

This led to an immediate stand-off. It was only broken after I pointed out to this otherwise reasonable doctor that there was a car park, in full view from his office where I was sitting, with a row of used Land Rover ambulances, many in perfectly good nick but for some relatively minor spare parts which could be sourced locally with our funding. This would be much quicker, cheaper and more environment friendly than his proposal. An enthusiastic endorsement of this from Mona, accompanied by her threat to withdraw her offer to lead this project, was enough to convince the Permanent Secretary to concur.

I am pleased to record that within twelve months we had the clinics fully up and running, the ambulances reconditioned and on call. Even in that relatively short time, statistics showed the number of births at UTH had dropped by some 25 per cent, with an equivalent number of healthy deliveries attributed to the health clinic network we had established. I understand that this project was taken up as an example of best practice by World

Bank public health experts for use in other similar situations. Bravo Mona and her missionary colleagues!

I am also happy to recall that many of the 400 or so Irish missionaries, whose predecessors had arrived with or just after the British pioneers who settled this part of central Africa at the end of the nineteenth century, became our friends. It was comforting when travelling around this vast country to know that there was a warm Irish welcome at each of the many mission stations that dotted even the more remote parts; I always travelled with a bottle of Irish whiskey stowed in the boot to share with them, come sundown.

One of the most interesting trips I made was to the far reaches of the Western Province, almost to the source of the mighty Zambesi river itself, from which the country took its name. I was a guest of the Capuchin Fathers who had a mission and school in Mongu, the provincial capital. From there we journeyed half a day up river by boat to a mission station beyond Kalabo, overlooking the border with Angola and only accessible from the river. Bowled over by the emotion of the moment, I unfurled an Irish flag and handed it over to the Capuchin Friar living in this remote spot.

A local urchin ran up to my host and tugged at his knotted rope belt. 'Father, Father, when will we have another movie to watch?' he asked excitedly. Without hesitation, my friend replied, 'Oh, Jonathan, any time from now.' Jonathan ran away happily to convey this news to his companions. Father then turned to me and explained that they never really knew when a movie would be sent out to them and that the hope and anticipation was such that it sustained morale indefinitely! Yes, these visits were a continual learning experience.

Likewise, Siobhán and I operated an open home in Lusaka for anyone who needed a bed or wished to relax in the pool or to engage in mortal combat on the tennis court. I still remember the first time a rather fetching Sister of Charity nervously asked if she could have a swim. We said yes, of course, but shortly there-after I was banished to the other side of the house until she was once again modestly robed. So it isn't true that I ever saw a nun in a swimsuit! (Mary Rose, my lips are sealed.)

We both enjoyed immensely our blood-sport Sunday evening bridge games with the Kiltegans based nearby. Siobhán's partner was the unique, irreplaceable, Eugene O'Reilly from Carrickmacross, County Monaghan; mine was the deceptively mild-mannered gambler, the late, great, much-lamented Julian Connolly.

Alas, both died suddenly and too soon; saintly deaths for good men who gave their best for others. I hope both are fondly remembered still in the Lusaka townships in which they worked. So many of our missionaries died prematurely; in memory of each, I say, *Ar dheis Dé go raibh se, dilis*.

One thing that many of us in Ireland share is a preoccupation with weather and listening to weather forecasts. We do love to talk about the weather and to comment both on our own and on others' predictions of same.

So it was hardly surprising, dear reader, that one of the things I missed most from watching Zambian television – this was also in the days before satellite dishes – was the absence of a local weather forecast after the news.

We had arrived in the month of April; I had an opportunity early on to meet with the Director General of Zambia National Broadcasting Corporation, ZNBC, as he wanted to visit Ireland to discuss a technical assistance programme for his staff (he subsequently had a successful trip which ended with IPA providing the training he wanted and some equipment from RTÉ sources). I took the opportunity to raise with him my concerns; could ZNBC not provide a simple weather forecast to assist viewers and listeners, as most national broadcasters worldwide did?

He chuckled heartily. Then, for he was a kindly soul, he gently pointed out that we were in the middle of the 'dry season', which usually lasted from April to October, when as I surely well knew by then, the sun rose at six in the morning and set at six in the evening. So, why would they waste time broadcasting that tomorrow the sun would once again shine all over the country all day?

He went on to explain that my desires would be met once the 'rainy season' arrived, usually starting at end of October and lasting, with luck, until towards the end of March, with a full weather forecast service appearing every morning and evening, tracking approaching weather systems. I still blush when I think of this, although my fascination with watching the weather forecast when they were eventually broadcast never diminished!

Before I end this chapter, I must recall our most famous visitor of all, not a politician or a person of pomp but our very own neighbour from Dalkey, the writer Maeve Binchy. Maeve and her delightful spouse, Gordon, visited Zambia in mid-1982. What a privilege!

In fact, Maeve had been a colleague of my father, Horace, in the London office of *The Irish Times* since the mid-1970s.

To digress briefly, my Dad had left school at age 15 in the mid-1930s to work in the Advertisement Department of *The Irish Times*, then under the inimitable editorship of one R. M. 'Bertie'

Smyllie. Dad was one of the first Roman Catholics to be employed by this pillar of the Anglo-Irish Protestant establishment. He had been obliged to do so as his own father, John Denham, was a bit of a philanderer, gambling family fortunes on bogus share investments and theatre holdings, for example, the Belfast Empire Theatre. Most of these proved to be worthless investments, going south early on in the infamous 'crash' of 1929.

My father served in The Irish Press group in the 1950s alongside Douglas Gageby, father of distinguished Supreme Court Justice Susan, who subsequently married into a different branch of the Denham clan. Douglas went on to become without doubt the most distinguished Editor of *The Irish Times* in the modern era.

By the mid-1970s, Dad was a fixture in the London Office and a firm friend and, dare I say, mentor to Maeve, whose writing ambitions he encouraged. Maeve, Gordon and Liam White, photographer, landed in Zambia with relatively little notice apart from an alert from my Dad to look after the three of them. In those days, communication with HQ was by telex machine (remember those? – they made a staccato sound, like a hyperdrive morse code machine) and DFA did not have either the ambition or the wherewithal to 'control' output from its officers. How times have changed!

Maeve's visit, a report of which appeared in *The Irish Times* on 7 September 1982, was a whirlwind of fun and laughter! Two events I recall illustrate this. The first was an unscheduled visit to the Monze convent of the Sisters of Charity, caused by Maeve's urgent need to respond to a call of nature. Screeching to a halt, I jumped out of the car to help her down from the Range Rover, ring the bell and let the good sisters know why we were there. But by the time I got around to her side of the car, Maeve had already leapt out while we were still moving and rushed in through the front door past a startled nun saying without pause in her stride, 'Hellosister!ImMaevemayiuseyourloopleasethanks.'

The second happening occurred in our living room later that evening over a glass of wine. Maeve had warned me earlier that she was expecting an important call from London and did I mind if she took it at our house. Telephone calls, as I remarked earlier, were significant events to be cherished, and which required advance booking and timing. Sure enough, the phone rang at the appointed time. Maeve excused herself and went into the next room to take the call. A few minutes later, she returned, slightly flushed, and said, 'Gordon, that was a literary agent in London. *Light a Penny Candle* has been accepted for publication so I think we will have enough money to get the kitchen done!' Maeve and Gordon had just moved into Pollyvilla in Dalkey before their African safari.

Light a Penny Candle was the first of Maeve's many highly acclaimed novels that launched her career as an internationally renowned writer; I like to think, therefore, that Siobhán and I have a small footnote in Irish literary history. When my Dad died all too suddenly in January 1984 on his way to work in *The Irish Times* London office (he had just rushed, as per usual for him, to jump aboard a London double-decker when he had a massive heart attack), Maeve wrote a beautiful elegy, a small extract of which is:

> It's over twelve years since I came to London and began my morning chats with Horace Denham. He had tales of people I never met and news of people I had. There seemed to be hardly anyone in the advertising business or in publishing that he didn't know. And it was all reciprocated. All over the

place people would ask me did I know him whenever I said that I worked for *The Irish Times*…. And for me this morning, it will be a lonely office without my morning conversations with a kind and courteous man whose delight in people lit up his face and his heart.

Maeve and Gordon will forever remain in my heart as the two most wonderful VIPs we had the good fortune to know.

Chapter 3

Brussels

Our Third Presidency at the coal face; the Irish Civil Service in microcosm, warts and all; Mexico, Pakistan, India and Thailand; Belgium, snow deliveries.

This is a short but not very happy chapter, reflecting a stressful period for the family.

A Belgian diplomat colleague once joked to me that 'the weather is awful, dank, damp, cold and wet in winter and humid, wet in summer'; she was talking about Ireland! If that is true of Ireland, how much more true, in spades as they say, is the miserable climate, summer and winter, of what has become our vaunted European capital. At least we have westerly winds that blow through constantly to move the rain on. Brussels air is dank, stuffy and stale in its oppressiveness.

Also, Brussels has proceeded to knock down a significant part of its heritage and to build some of the worst horticultural hot-house style structures in which to place the European Commission, the Council and the European Parliament, presumably on the pretext that they will be encouraged to grow into wisdom! Let us hope that there is adequate ventilation, that watchword of the recent pandemic, to take away all that hot air these institutions generate!

I often wonder if the European Union would be a more compatible, socially aware, kinder, gentler institution if it were at home in a larger, more emotionally mature and self-confident environment like Paris or Milan or Madrid? Or Stockholm?

What a truly depressed city Brussels has become, with the ethnic Brusselois evidently resentful of their foreign guests, landlords laying down impossible rules for tenants, the pervasive odour of waffle stands and drivers bent on taking out their passive-aggressive behaviour on other road users. The EU just hasn't got the message at all.

The occasion of my being in Brussels was a request put to me late in 1983, while working still in the tranquil confines of the Publications Section at HQ, then part of the Anglo-Irish Division propaganda wing. I was asked if I would be interested in moving for a year, strictly time-bound, beginning in January 1984, to assist in our Third EU Presidency which would run from July to December. Of course I said yes without hesitation, then went home in a state of great excitement to break the news to my poor, long-suffering spouse who was just getting used to being home from our four-year African safari and who now had three children, including our baby daughter, Andrea, to cope with, as well as a newly acquired house in Dalkey to furnish.

I suppose the opportunity was one neither of us felt I could refuse, so off I set, in mid-winter, exchanging lowering grey cloud, pelting rain and the sharp dampness of Dublin for that cold, wet, miserable city that is the European hub, Brussels. Leaving aside the nil-nil draw in climate, Brussels has, without a shadow of a doubt, the most malign landlord system in my quite extensive global experience at this stage. Not only did colleagues frighten me with tales of lost deposits and other horrors, but what the local estate agents showed me that winter brought on a major rethink on whether this was a smart move on my part.

Eventually, I did find a half-way decent semi-detached house, quite newly built by a Moroccan trader who himself lived in what was even then a mainly North African populated ghetto of Schaerbeek. His property investment was in the Flemish-speaking neighbourhood of St. Stevens Woluwe, near Zaventem, within sight of NATO. Though I didn't fully appreciate it at the time, the linguistic designation was all-important from a local perspective. For obvious reasons, most of my colleagues lived in Walloon, that is, French-speaking, districts.

The house itself was certainly adequate but no more; it would do us for the year that was in it. It wasn't particularly near to anywhere, not shops, schools or public transport, so I also invested, thanks to a departmental car loan, in a VW Golf. That was probably one of the best decisions and I was sorry at the end of the year to let it go.

Siobhán and the three children moved over a short time later. We had assumed our two eldest would have places in the European School but, alas, that was not so simple. Because we were arriving mid-academic year, only one place could be guaranteed. So we were faced with the difficult decision of whether to start our eldest daughter in the nearest French-speaking school available, across the beltway and across the linguistic divide. Four months of tears every morning followed as I left Aisling to school and headed in to work. Only after the new school year started did we acquire a place for her in the European School, by then more than a tad late. I always feared we had traumatised her beyond redemption, but it seems not.

To add to our family misery, our beautiful baby daughter, Andrea, just a year old, developed a horrific cough and wheeze which came close to turning into pneumonia. She required both hospital and specialist visits and an intensive round of physiotherapy, not easy for such a young infant and certainly not easy for her parents to observe.

We had daily morning meetings in the Irish Mission in the six months before as well as during the Presidency, so I had a chance early on to get to know my colleagues, both from Foreign Affairs and other departments. They were, without exception, all lovely people, competent in their 'chosen subject' and good company throughout my time in Brussels. We had a restaurant close to the mission where we would congregate for lunch when able to do so; the food and the décor were unremarkable, but the conversation was always stimulating.

I was assigned to help one of the two DFA Counsellors at the Mission. His brief included relations with all Third Countries (known as the 113 Committee-External Relations) and I was told to mind India, Mexico, Pakistan, the ASEAN countries and Sri Lanka. A colleague and I were to help with a major renegotiation of the Lomé Convention (Lomé III) which spelt out the EC's trade and financial relationship with Africa, Caribbean & Pacific (mainly former British and French colonial) nations. I had worked under Garret Fitzgerald's leadership on Lomé I in our first Presidency in 1975, and managed to avoid the first renewal negotiations in 1979 (Lomé II) thanks to the department not paying sufficient attention to its personnel record-keeping, a perennial hazard.

The Lomé negotiations were slow and tedious. It was part of the normal pattern of international negotiations, especially where the EU is concerned, which usually involves the interests of some Member States more than others, but where every MS insists on its right to be consulted. Cards are played close to the Commission's ample bosom and hands are not revealed until the last moment – and beyond. Thus, there are seemingly endless periods of *ennui* and inactivity, of sheer, mind-numbing boredom where one wishes one had picked up the skills of lighthouse keepers to while away time.

Mexico

On the brighter side in that year, my work took me to places as far flung as Mexico City, Rawalpindi, New Delhi and Bangkok. Mexico City impressed with its over-and-under highways in the middle of an earthquake zone, its sanitised 'Zona Rosa' shopping area and the dire, dirt-laden poverty of its mountainside shanty towns. It was also home to those strange pre-Vatican II Legionaries of Christ, prevalent and powerful in their smart cassocks and ultra-white dog collars.

There was one remarkable Irishman there, a scion of the De La Rue currency-printing family company. His name now escapes me, but he took us on an unforgettable and absolutely fascinating tour of the Chapultepec National Museum of Anthropology. What started as a private tour with three of us in tow quickly snowballed into a crowd of over 20 as he revealed its marvels, many of which he had had a personal hand in discovering. I regret I never got to thank him properly for his kindness.

My other memory of Mexico is the wonderful ceremony held every year to honour the St Patricio Irish battalion which fought

alongside the Mexicans at The Alamo and who were subsequently hunted down and destroyed by Texan forces. Yet again, it is an
example of the worldwide influence of our little country. While
on the subject of Mexico-Irish relations, I should mention that
our Honorary Consul of Ireland for many years was an extremely wealthy Spanish multi-millionaire who employed a minion
to handle any consular issues and who, like the vast majority
of Honorary Consuls the world over, enjoyed the prestige and
social standing of the title without necessarily having any emo-
tional attachment (John Keane in Seattle being an honourable
exception; see Chapter 7). He became very friendly with a former Taoiseach and eventually went into exile, I gather, due to a
regime change in Mexico.

Pakistan

I recall being impressed by Pakistan, the imposing backdrop
of the mighty, snow-drenched Himalayas contrasted with the
starkly modern but clean and efficient capital city of Islamabad
and its dusty, colourful, historic neighbour, Rawalpindi. Carpet
bazaars could keep one fascinated for years, if permitted, and
were a learning experience in the traditions of this vast mountain
hinterland.

Our Pakistani guides were courteous and generous in their
hospitality. A trip to another ancient city in Kashmir, Lahore, was
particularly fascinating, taking in the enormous Red Mosque,
the mysterious, magical Bazaar which seemed to go on forever.
Danger loomed, not from the massed throngs of humanity that
inhabited the bazaar, all of whom were unfailingly courteous,
but from the complex web of stalls, the seemingly endless maze
that bedazzled and bewildered those lacking a strong sense of

direction or good memory of paths taken. We did get out eventually, laden with treasures and spices to rival The Three Kings! Or so it seemed at the time; I regret now not being even more avaricious and of not taking this unique opportunity to export more oriental delights!

The fabled Shalimar Gardens were another wonder to behold; tranquil, serene, seductive are descriptions that come to mind, of the likes of Xanadu in Coleridge's *Kublai Khan* or Kipling's descriptions of the North West Frontier. It seemed strange to be in such a beautiful place yet so near the epicentre of a conflict zone that was the disputed India-Pakistan border. I have a photograph of a large Briggs & Stratton roller mower being hauled across the lawns harnessed to an oxen – local ingenuity in the face of adversity (in this case, lack of fuel) triumphed yet again. I liked Pakistan and would love to visit it again sometime. It is a pity that it has been so tarnished at a geopolitical level, bullied by large countries with their own interests and now, at international level, a bit like a dog that has got itself a bad name for biting. But a 'failed state' it is not; it is one of the civilised societies of this world.

India

India is another beautiful, bustling, bewitching country, full of teeming chaos but always muddling through in the end. Indians like to please and to be accepted with respect. Dignity is important and that can cause them to be prickly at times, especially at official level. My visit with the 113 Committee from Brussels in 1984 started with great pomp and not a little formality. The literal piles of files and paperwork and the number of headless-chicken-like bodies moving the piles around in Dickensian government offices has to be seen to be believed. The only other place I have ever come across such bureaucracy was in the United Nations!

Fortunately, some Irish informality, a large dose of flattery and charm, and a great deal of patience achieved the desired result, with India signing a new memorandum of understanding which would consolidate reasonably good trading relations, at the time at least.

A delightful Delhi hotel and some good Kingfisher local beer eased the pain of long, wearisome negotiations. Delhi has some stunning Lutyens architecture from imperial times and a fascinating open market in old Delhi where we had some of the tastiest food in the city, and without any undesirable consequences (yes, okay, I do have a strong digestive system and am not known for suffering when dining for Ireland). Likewise, a day off to visit the Red Fort and the Taj Mahal, with my own moment in front of it, were highlights I shall forever remember.

India would also be high on my list of places I would have liked to have spent more time exploring. A posting would certainly have been enjoyed but I was in the wrong postings cycle and it never became vacant at the right moment, alas.

Thailand

Most people visit Thailand for vacations; I went to attend a meeting with ASEAN (a South East Asian countries grouping, modelled on the EU with all its worst bureaucratic tendencies!) and to visit what was the world's largest pineapple factory, based in Cha Am, the west coast of Thailand that no one ever visits. But I did get to sample Bangkok, then still just about navigable by car and fascinating for its temples, floating restaurants and nightlife along Paipong Road; oh, and Thompson's silk shop.

Painting of Sanderstead All Saints Church, Surrey, where I spent my formative teen years.

On the Howth Road, Killester, 1951, carrying a blackthorn stick used in 1916.

The Ireland stand, John Fisher School, Purley, Surrey, 1966, with my Mum, Dad and sisters.

The happy couple with Rev Brendan Heffernan, August 1973.

A clipping of Ireiand's first EU Presidency, January 1975.
An arrow points to the author.

For H.E. Mr D. Denham

We thank you for your contribution to our growth. God bless & keep smiling all the way.

14th August,

KD

A signed photograph of the author
and President of Zambia, Dr. Kenneth Kaunda.

Laying a wreath at the Robert Emmet statue.

Meeting President Reagan at The White House.

Mary Robinson at the Victoria Falls.

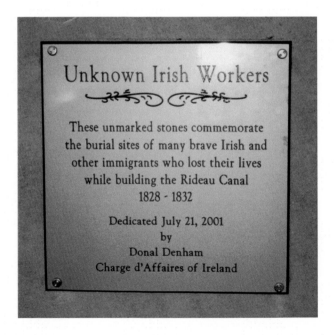

Unknown Irish Workers

These unmarked stones commemorate
the burial sites of many brave Irish and
other immigrants who lost their lives
while building the Rideau Canal
1828 - 1832

Dedicated July 21, 2001
by
Donal Denham
Charge d'Affaires of Ireland

Plaque commemorating Irish workers who died
while building the Rideau Canal in Ottawa.

Atop the Golden Gate Bridge – a definite highlight.

With former US Secretary of State
George Schultz.

TWH Spokeswoman!

With Martin Sheen and Merv Griffin.

With an injured Colin Farrell at the Oscars in LA.

A proud Butte, Montana miner.

Our Lady of the Rockies, Butte, Montana.

Our just-opened five-star luxury hotel in Cha Am, courtesy of ASEAN, was deserted despite being the 'pineapple capital of the world', with an enormous factory around which we were proudly given a tour. Cha Am lies on the main arm of Thailand, heading towards Malaysia, opposite to its much more famous tourist destination, Pattaya. So, apart from my fellow bureaucrats, it made for an almost dull anti-climax after the sights and sounds of Bangkok, a rather stilted, solemn occasion. We got the business done, made our hosts happy and went home to Brussels for Christmas. I was almost glad to experience the cold, dark, dank dampness of that dull city.

Meanwhile, in between my global peregrinations, EU negotiations with the ACP (African, Caribbean, Pacific nations), presided over on our side by the Irish Presidency, continued on their tedious way with long nights and line by line battles over draft wording long after people had forgotten why they were there in the first place!

We all knew, in any event, that according to the style and traditions of the European Commission, our true masters, there would be little or no progress on most issues until the aid money offer underwriting Lomé had been decided upon. Until then, we had countless texts, often contradictory, full of square brackets, round brackets, *guimets* (brackets in French), italics, bold text and all in at least two working languages, English and French, which created their own difficulties with slightly different linguistic nuances, for example, sensitive vs *sensibile*. No one ever claimed that negotiating on behalf of 10 with 46 on the other side of the table was going to be easy!

The Commission, in league as ever with its German paymasters and British and French ex-colonial masters, were, understandably, disinclined to reveal any aid figure before the other parts of the draft convention had been agreed; this tied at least one hand behind our collective backs and added greatly to stress levels. It also provided a classic Catch-22 scenario. This game of draft charades was only finally broken by a highly restricted marathon Foreign Ministers-only session, lasting most of the night after an early start and only days before Heads of State were due to meet once more in Lomé to sign off on the negotiations. Needless to say, my mid-level colleagues and I spent the night sitting outside closed doors drinking interminable cups of awful, artificial milk-laden coffee to stay awake.

With a dramatic flourish to rival the Vatican's white smoke announcements, our elegant, esteemed Minister for Foreign Affairs of the day, always dapper, emerged, bright-eyed and bushy-tailed to announce that a figure had been agreed, more generous than the Commission had originally offered but less than the ACP had sought, which would secure everyone's signature on a new Convention at Lomé. The Irish Presidency duly took credit for yet another diplomatic victory, a major triumph in 1984.

Christmas that year was spent with my parents in London, always delighted and excited to have their grandchildren present for such a celebration, full of traditional atmosphere as only the British can make the season of good cheer. But our return to Brussels saw orders to pack up and leave as quickly as possible as the Presidency was over, and our permanent Brussels-based colleagues wanted their offices back and a return to normality as soon as we could manage it. What Irish officialdom didn't reckon with was the fall of nearly a foot of snow in one icy blast which brought the city to a halt amid sub-zero Arctic temperatures.

It also coincided with the Beverly Smyth removals van, sent out to pick up our belongings and those of several other temporarily assigned families. We were first on their list, however the engine, not used to such extreme conditions, promptly seized up overnight right in front of our house. We ended up providing refuge, food and a bed to the two frozen staff that came with the truck while they did their best to find replacement parts. Fortunately for them, we had by that stage almost a family relationship with the company who never let us down over all those years of moving our bits and pieces, goods and chattels, around the globe.

When we eventually got home at the end of January, 1985, it was pleasant to experience the balmy winter days of dear old Dublin after Brussels' bleak midwinter snows. I didn't know, however, what tragedy awaited just days ahead.

Chapter 4

Washington, DC

An Editor! The Centre of the Political Universe; on the Beltway, off the Beltway, such is life; Reagan, his last two years, the first two of Bush the Elder; creating an economic lobby for Ireland Inc; 3/17 inside the Oval Office; a Tale of Two Banks (WB & IMF); Jim Power, mentor and monk; agriculture, as ever a French preserve; Air Force 2, Charles J. Haughey and his amazing Arabian stallions.

1985: Publications Editor

In the middle of a snowy, extremely cold winter, the family packed up once more and moved home from Brussels. We left behind a deep-frozen city to rediscover an ever-windy Dalkey. And I took up my previous role as Editor of Publications at HQ.

The year 1985 started off sadly; Dad was a wonderful father and a great, kind person (see kind words Maeve Binchy wrote about him at the end of Chapter 2). Maeve and Dad were close colleagues in the London office of *The Irish Times*. Dad never paid much attention to the gulf between journalists and 'commercial types' who cohabit in most media organisations. He was always able to bridge the divide and relate on a human level.

It was a Monday, 28 January, a nice sunny winter morning, I recall, when the phone on my desk rang shortly after 10.00 am. It was a London policeman with a strong cockney accent. There was no easy way to soften the hammer blow news that Dad had died shortly after jumping on to a London Bus in The City, late for a meeting with an ad agency; a massive heart attack, dead on arrival at St. Thomas' Hospital. I knew he had been having some leg-related circulation problems but had no idea it was symptomatic of a more serious issue. He was a dapper gent, diminutive but with an infectious laugh and a way of bringing a smile to the gloomiest face.

His childhood in the 1930s had been pretty brutal, one of six children with a father who died when he was still a teenager. He left the Catholic University School, run by Marists, after a minimal education and began his career with *The Irish Times* collecting what were called 'classified' and 'small ads' which graced the title bar and back pages in those days. He used to talk about endless walks up and down Grafton Street to encourage advertisers and to collect their copy, punctuated by a morning tea break either in Bewleys or Brown Thomas or, occasionally, Fullers. He subsequently joined *The Irish Press* (though not a Dev supporter) and became firm friends with Douglas Gageby, who was without a peer in the Irish editorial demesne. Douglas brought my Dad back to *The Irish Times* in 1960 when he assumed the Editor's chair. It was the highlight of Dad's career and he was bursting with pride – and devotion and commitment –when appointed as Group Advertisement Manager. That appointment lasted until Major T.B. McDowell arrived on the scene and took absolute personal control of the business.

The early 1960s were an exciting time at *The Irish Times*, with their takeover of the venerable Dublin *Evening Mail* and turning it into Ireland's first 'tabloid' format newspaper. Likewise, they bought and developed the *Radio Review* which became the precursor of the *RTÉ Guide* as Irish television arrived in 1961. RTÉ saw the immense revenue potential of a weekly TV magazine and basically forced *The Irish Times* to relinquish the *Radio Review* in favour of the *Guide*. An attempt to create a tabloid Sunday paper almost succeeded with the launch of the *Sunday Review*, first of its kind to use colour and to have a children's cartoon supplement, but again, the cut-throat competition from both Independent and Press newspaper groups forced it to fold by 1964. At that time, Dublin had three morning newspapers, three evening papers and the Sunday market was dominated by *The Sunday Press*. Ironically, with the addition of some spicy 'page 3' photos and stories, the *Sunday World* would emerge to outsell all its rivals. *The Irish Times* management in the early 1960s was progressive before its time.

Dad's passing in 1985 was marked by a large funeral service back in Dublin in February and many nice, consoling tributes to his work and character; Maeve Binchy wrote two poignant pieces which are treasured by the family.

I had returned to Publications, then part of Anglo-Irish Division overseen by Margaret Hennessy, a kind and considerate officer. Recalling my Dad's role in those halcyon days in the 1960s, I embarked on a thorough modernisation of the department's publications, our monthly magazine, *Ireland Today*, and our other occasional *Facts About Ireland* and *Aspects of Ireland* series.

I had a great team to support this endeavour. Firstly there was Geoffrey Keating (who rose to become an excellent Ambassador and a close friend) and Tom Hanney (likewise), and subsequently the late Dr Maurice Roche who, it turned out, had an amazing business talent and was responsible for turning our loss-making unit into a commercial success! Maurice, who was from Cork and had a degree in Theology (he was Church of Ireland) died tragically in October 2003 from a fall off a horse; riding was his passion. Maurice subsequently left the Department of Foreign Affairs. The DFA has never been good at holding on to people of real talent; if I hadn't intervened, it would have lost the brilliant Director of the Passport Office, too. Maurice became Special Advisor to the Tánaiste, Mary Harney, and a linchpin of the then Fianna Fáil–Progressive Democrats coalition government, one of the best we've ever had, in my humble opinion.

The redesign and branding of our publications was brilliantly executed by Bill Murphy & Associates and won first place in its category in that year's Kilkenny Design Awards, though the department hardly acknowledged that accolade.

Maurice also managed to pre-sell an unprecedented 5,000 copies of a new edition of *Facts About Ireland*, which topped the Irish bestseller list for a record six weeks. *Facts* was fiendishly difficult to put together since both photos and details went out of date so quickly, plus the publication was stalled by an innate reluctance to publish anything relating to Northern Ireland. A decision to go ahead had to be dragged out tooth and nail. It was ever thus with our Anglo-Irish Division, even hiding secrets from one another; classic left hand, right hand syndrome.

Needless to add, the profits from our publication went straight into the exchequer so the department didn't benefit directly from Maurice's initiative and none of us got any credit for our collective efforts. *C'est la vie.*

Later in the year I was asked to take over as Deputy Chief of Protocol from Brian Nason who had been appointed as Consul General San Francisco and who subsequently became the husband of Geraldine Byrne, at that time serving her first stint in New York. My boss as Chief was Declan Connolly with whom I had worked in Brussels; small world, indeed. However, I hardly had time to adjust – Protocol is one of the best jobs at HQ since it involves meeting interesting people, fine dining and not too much paperwork!

The one noteworthy experience I recall while there were the Anglo-Irish negotiations at Officials level which alternated between Belfast, London and Dublin, invariably over a discreet but lavish dinner in Iveagh House, usually in the Secretary General's anteroom or equivalent. I organised the food and drink, the best of the wines and cognac that our Iveagh House cellars possessed. More's the pity an excellent, long-accumulated collection of fine wines, kept in perfect conditions in the eighteenth century barrel vaults of Iveagh House, were targeted by populist media and the department was pressured into selling it off in the name of political correctness. One trick I learned early on from these occasions was to collect the menu cards on which the British side often used to scribble down notes. I used to send these up to Anglo-Irish colleagues the following morning.

A footnote in history came with the signing of the 1985 Agreement on Northern Ireland. The night before the signing in Hillsborough, itself a destination shrouded in the most secrecy both sides could apply, I was given the final version of the unsigned agreement and asked to jump in a taxi, fly to London and travel to the Foreign and Commonwealth Office (FCO). There I was to have it ribboned and sealed, and to apply our ribbon and seal to their version once both had been checked to ensure they were identical. This I did, in a room in the bowels of the FCO.

I never saw the fancy part and returned to Dublin carrying their version and handed it over to Anglo-Irish. I travelled out to Baldonnel very early the following morning and we waved goodbye to Garret and Peter Barry as they boarded a Shorts twin propeller leased from Aer Lingus, bound for what we were told was to be Belfast. It was an interesting and intriguing moment.

1986: Washington, DC

Ever one for a foreign adventure, I applied for and was offered a First Secretary post in our Washington, DC Embassy in early 1986. It was ostensibly as Press Officer, but another officer, already in situ, was given the role shortly before I arrived there in March 1986. Not that I minded one bit; working as Economic First Secretary held great potential and meant working with a very pleasant, gentle person who basically allowed me to do my own thing from day one.

Washington is a fascinating place, a city of political intrigue without parallel, dominated by the 'inside the Beltway' gossip and rumour machine as defined by the massive orbital highway that defined whether you were in the political loop ... or out of it. The equivalent 'outside the Beltway' was a badge of honour awarded to the rest of the United States, seen as normal but dull people and, most significantly and patronisingly, as ignorant outsiders. Donald Trump would thrive on that.

Even more discriminating were the areas of the city in which one lived or did not. Divided into four quadrants, three of which were primarily black and poor ghettos, only the Northwest was deemed an appropriate residential address for the rich, the powerful and foreign nationals. And within that area, Georgetown is the Ballsbridge of DC. Washington, however, is essentially located on land carved out from the confluence of the states of Virginia and Maryland at the mighty Potomac River. And the less powerful tend to live in places like Bethesda Maryland, a rather bland neighbourhood.

The more discerning among us chose to live across the river in Northern Virginia, more specifically, McLean, home territory of the Kennedy clan. My daily commute, a mere 15–20 minutes most days, took me across the excitingly narrow Chain Bridge with stunning views of the raging torrents of the Potomac far below. Ambassador McKernan, never shy when it came to a waspish comment, dismissed our location as 'out in the boonies'.

But he was quite mistaken. McLean provided us with an idyllic family existence, a visually stunning setting during the different seasons, easy access to places beyond The Beltway, an excellent school and parish in St. John's and a close-knit expatriate community network which made every moment a delight.

My work developed apace as we concentrated on developing an economic support network with Irish American staffers in Congress (the politicians themselves we left to the Embassy A Team to avoid upsetting them). In fact, it was staffers on the Ways & Means Committee who had more influence over getting items on or off the agenda and who could wield power to influence decisions.

No better example than this was the defence campaign we mounted in 1988-89 to protect our low international tax policy for multinationals against the attentions of both the Senate Finance Committee and the House Ways & Means Committee as they struggled to get their acts together in pursuit of a share of foreign earnings of US companies. Yes, it was an active issue back then also (in those days, we had a preferential 10 per cent tax rate for foreign investment which changed to 12.5 per cent for all shortly thereafter, to deflect criticism of positive discrimination). A concerted effort from Team Ireland, led by the Embassy 'B Team', aided and abetted by Industry & Commerce, IDA Ireland and Enterprise Ireland, managed to stymie a rather chaotic effort from the Democratic-controlled House Ways & Means, and to drive a wedge between it and the Senate Finance crowd, which had many Republicans among its members. It was such challenging and interesting work, very satisfying to have such an opportunity.

Another lobbying issue which was a continual battle was our defence of casein exports to the US, mainly on behalf of the Irish Dairy Board and the Kerry Group, though they were fierce competitors who had to be handled separately and with great care! Casein, I should explain, is a lucrative, semi-magical waste product where the curd is taken from the whey in cheese production. Ireland's ever-resourceful, lean and mean dairy industry discovered that casein was a remarkable binding agent, the secret ingredient that holds together, at least until opened, the cream and the whiskey in the spectacular success story that is Bailey's Irish Cream and spin-off imitators. And casein is also, among its other applications, the basis for non-dairy (powdered) coffee creamer and for white glue (for example, Elmer's in the US).

The US dairy industry in the 1950s had, rather short-sightedly as it turned out, declined to produce casein as it was not in receipt of a federal US Department of Agriculture (USDA) subsidy to do so. So, it was left to Ireland and our rival New Zealand dairy industry to meet a virtually insatiable demand for casein in the US market. And to join with a professional lobby group of importers in a fight with the extremely powerful US dairy lobby who were continually attempting to convince both the USDA and Congress to adopt regulations to raise the tariff on casein imports. What a tussle we had! It was a great experience in showing how Congress works, or more importantly, can be blocked from working, a far easier task. Frequent appearances as an observer in congressional committees proved to be fascinating, watching the different dynamics and undercurrents at work behind the scenes.

I also learned to be an expert in finding my way around the corridors of US power, the labyrinth of underground tunnels, including a driverless railway linking the Senate with the House, and the plethora of office buildings in which senators and representatives and their many staff resided. In particular, and well before 9/11 of course, I recall walking on a crisp autumnal evening under an archway outside the Senate when a tall and bulky individual loomed before me. It was no less than the ever-substantial figure of Ted Kennedy. Where else in the world could you say '*Dia dhuit*, Good evening, Senator!' to one of the most famous of politicians of his era, with no more than a shadow between you?

Autumn in DC, or the fall as they say, was spectacular, a veritable riot of red-hued tones, from dark brown to bright yellow. To walk from Key Bridge (named after the patriot who wrote the *Star Spangled Banner*) to the steps of the Capitol building, pausing along the way to admire the Lincoln Memorial, Vietnam Wall (Vietnam Veterans Memorial), the Reflecting Pool and nearby Tidal Basin and Jefferson Memorial to the right, the White House in the distance on your left, past the Washington Monument along The Mall flanked by a phalanx of museums that make up the Smithsonian Institution (the Air & Space will always be my enduring favourite) is simply a unique privilege. To sit on the grassy knoll in front of the Washington Memorial with a picnic on the Fourth of July, surrounded by our children and many others of that great nation's own, watching a magnificent fireworks display, is something I will forever treasure.

But back to work! One of our first distinguished visitors was Gemma Hussey, Minister for Social Welfare and her junior Minister in Labour and in Education, Enda Kenny. They came to study a new and controversial concept of the day, 'workfare', which obliged the unemployed to work on communal projects in exchange for welfare payments. Remember, Ireland's unemployment scaled the heights of 20 per cent at one stage. Gemma was pleasant throughout and wrote me a nice thank you letter afterwards. Enda was also very decent and good company during their trip. On one occasion, driving along The Mall, he asked if we could pull over to take a quick look at the Vietnam Wall. This we did, and Enda walked along the panels, stopping before one and pointing to a name: 'There he is, Donal; I was at school with him. Now, I can tell his parents I saw his name here,' which I thought was a considerate and compassionate gesture for him to make.

That visit took us (I was the assigned Embassy escort) to the rather unusual state of West Virginia, a depressed area ravaged by defunct coal mines but a proud 'hillbilly' community. Senator Robert Byrd was one of our hosts, a mighty powerful politician both at federal and state level.

All was going swimmingly with my Fine Gael visitors until Gemma insisted on eating shellfish at dinner and suffered the consequences. Our trip back to DC was fast and furious! Lunch the following day hosted by Ambassador McKernan was quite tense and Gemma disappeared back to her hotel early on and wasn't seen again until the run to the airport, no pun intended.

We had many such VIP visits during my time in Washington. Every Patrick's Day saw the annual pilgrimage of Taoisigh and Ministers for Foreign Affairs to pay homage, first of all to the incumbent in The White House, in this case, Ronald Reagan and then George H.W. Bush (a 'wasp' with little sympathy for Ireland at any level), and to the American-Irish congressional royalty, foremost of whom were Tip O'Neill and the Kennedy dynasty.

I was assigned the more remote duties – the Ancient Order of Hibernians dinner in Baltimore, the Custis Lee commemoration in Arlington, the Robert Emmet wreath-laying on Massachusetts Avenue – all enjoyable tasks and none that attracted much notice on the day of emerald green America. On St Patrick's Day, 1987, Reagan had just received the Irish delegation for the annual handing over of shamrock (pre-inspected by USDA and always delivered just in time without any soil attached, unlike the politicians). Brian Lenihan was the Minister as our government had just changed and Charlie Haughey was back in power. And we had a great team of administrative support staff, among which was Karen Coyne. Karen was a championship-winning Irish dancer, among her many talents, and taught both our daughters Aisling and Andrea in her spare time, bringing them up to a level where they were among the Irish dancers who participated in the St. Patrick's Day Parade along The Mall in 1988, much to the delight of their proud parents who were with the Irish Delegation on the Reviewing Stand that day! Such were Karen's skills and determination that she subsequently returned to DC a few years after her DFA posting had ended, finding a key administrative post in the International Monetary Fund.

I was given several lower-profile March 17 events to cover that first year in DC and felt relieved as I preferred to do the minor celebrations. I recall that I had just finished the nearby Robert Emmet statue ceremony and was taking time out in the Embassy when the phone rang. It was a Mrs. Owsley, 87 at the time and widow of the very first resident US Ambassador to Ireland. Mr. Owsley senior had made his money inventing something called the 'ball jar', a precursor to the tin can. Mrs. Owsley was a Top 100 donor to the Republican Party and as such, President Reagan had invited her to The White House that afternoon to recognise her contribution. Her 55-year-old son, Robert junior, was accompanying her and she wondered if someone from the Embassy would like to join them. Of course, *carpe diem*, I was the only one on the spot, so I said yes, I would be delighted.

An hour later, I was shaking hands with the President himself in the Oval Office, complete with shamrock bowl as the backdrop to a unique photo opportunity. I even ended up with a signed photo awhile later to prove it! It was a 30-second conversation, me muttering 'Hello, Mr. President, Happy St. Patrick's Day!' and Ronald saying, 'Oh yes, I met your guys earlier!' Exit stage right ...

My feat in making it two Irish visits to 1600 Pennsylvania Avenue in one day was not, unsurprisingly, fully appreciated. At our staff meeting the day after, sitting as usual in a semi-circle in front of the Ambassador – certain DFA bad habits die hard, among them 'morning prayers' – my unalloyed pleasure in briefing colleagues on the previous day's events was greeted with a put-down remark by the Ambassador about consorting with fat-cat Republicans.

My role as Agriculture Attaché had its interesting moments also. USDA organised a bi-annual trip for our diplomats group which took us that year to Iowa and Nebraska. Neither state had much profile in Irish American lore, but I did discover a connection with Ames, Iowa, home to a substantial agriculture research facility. One of the staff there was from Ireland on secondment from An Foras Talúntais/The Agricultural Institute (AFT). The friendliness of the locals in both states made up for the rather dreary landscape, endless fields of corn, punctuated by large grain storage towers and the occasional slaughterhouse for pigs, as pork was also big in Iowa and Nebraska.

Washington, DC also brought me into contact with the legendary Charles J. Haughey (CJH) on two occasions. The first was a donation of two Desert Arabian stallions from a wealthy art collector and horse breeder, Vincent Melzac, also former Director of the Corcoran Art Gallery in DC. This unusual bequest was made shortly before he died; Vincent was an admirer of Irish bloodstock and envisaged eventually breeding a cross with Connemara ponies from his Desert Arabian gift.

What neither Charlie nor the Department of Agriculture realised was that Arabian, as in sheiks riding wonderful golden thoroughbreds across the great desert under the stars, and Desert Arabian, were two distinct breeds and the latter did not conjure up such romantic images. Indeed, when I drove down to the Melzac ranch in Romney, West Virginia, I found a stable full of dun-coloured ponies, small and sturdy in stature, more work than racehorse. But the department in Dublin had their instructions from Kinsealy, and no one was prepared to tell Charlie the truth which was that the donation to the Irish National Stud in Kildare was unlikely to prove of any radical or enduring breeding value in the way he assumed.

So two senior officials flew out from Dublin and I escorted them to Romney to meet Sheila, Vincent's widow and faithful companion in his final moments. Sheila was a most decent woman in every respect and we had become firm friends over the months since Vincent had passed away. Romney was a rather remote spot, deep in the hills of West Virginia, and she enjoyed our company on both occasions. She allowed the two officials to choose the best two stallions from the bunch and we arranged their transfer to the National Stud, at considerable state expense. Sometime later, Sheila asked me for an update on how the two misfortunate animals were doing (she had pet names for the entire herd).

I duly made a call to Kildare and spoke to someone in charge. After first denying any knowledge of their existence, the official informed me that the stallions had been assessed and after due consideration it had been decided that they did not fit with the stud's breeding programme and had been banished to an annexe to live out the remainder of their lives in comfort as guests of Ireland. I did not have the heart to break the news to Sheila that all the trouble we had gone to in order to respect Vincent's wishes had been in vain. I just hope the two animals in question provided some value at the stud. And obviously Charles Haughey was never disabused of his dream of an Irish Arabian Gold Cup winner.

The second encounter with Haughey was face-to-face, during his St Patrick's Day visit to DC in 1990. He and his large entourage, by Irish standards, included arch-mandarin Padraig O hUiginn and the formidable P.J. Mara. Receiving a stare from either was like touching a live wire. Unusually for the Embassy's economic team, I had a small role to play in the visit. I had been involved in arranging for advice from the US Environmental Protection Agency, where I had built up contacts, to be given to Dublin in setting up our own agency in Ireland. As was his wont, Charlie had taken a personal interest in the issue, and as a result played a key hands-on role in the setup of an Irish EPA.

The mutual link was Bill McCummiskey whom I had be-friended in Zambia in the 1980s when he was in AFT who were leading a clean water project in Northern province. Bill was a gent and quite clever. He also knew how to navigate and ride our political system for the general good of the community. It was Bill who asked me to contact the EPA and who came to DC with CJH.

Haughey's final meeting before leaving DC after a couple of days of high-octane wining and dining at the highest reaches of US politics was with the Director General of the US EPA and I was assigned as note-taker. With some trepidation, I turned up at the appointed time at Blair House, the US official VIP guesthouse, just opposite The White House itself. As per usual, Haughey kept everyone waiting downstairs in the hall, car engines idling. I introduced myself to O'hUiginn and when Haughey swept down the stairs I was told to stick close. We travelled the ex-tremely short distance to the famous White House lawn for a last handshake between himself and Bush before we were all hustled aboard Air Force 1 and 2, enormous and exceptionally noisy he-licopters, for a spectacular low-level flight to Andrews Air Force Base where the Irish Government jet was waiting.

I was ushered into the presence of our Great One and introduced him to the EPA Director General who was waiting patiently in the Andrews departure guest lounge. All I remember is sitting opposite Charlie and beside the DG, nervously scribbling as quickly as I could as Charlie spoke in his usual gravelly, hushed tones, hooded eyelids famously drooped, as he shot staccato questions one after another at the DG. The poor man hardly knew what hit him! But it must have been a success as Bill, who had been beside CJH at our meeting, reported that Haughey had seemed pleased, as far as one could ever tell, with the outcome.

Having waved the jet off into a gloriously starry Washington night, I slumped, adrenalin rapidly draining, into the back of a generously provided limo for a ride back into town. That airforce sofa was as close as I ever wanted to be to that intimidating, spellbindingly brilliant St. Joseph's Marino prodigy, Charles J. Haughey. Whatever you may think of him, good or bad, he was a fascinating specimen of Irish politician.

The World Bank (WB) and the International Monetary Fund (IMF) both have their Headquarters in DC, located, of course, in luxury surroundings to which they both became accustomed long ago. A job in either institution was a passport to prosperity for any one lucky enough to obtain one. In fact, jobs are allocated by way of a system of national quotas, as I discovered when I visited both institutions to meet the Irish nationals working within each. The IMF Irish staff of the time were reserved and generally not interested in having a working relationship with the embassy, at least not at my grade (and the Ambassador had little or no time or interest in courting either them or World Bank staffers, it must be said).

The World Bank staff, on the other hand, were delighted that I had taken the initiative of introducing myself. We quickly established an informal WB network which was to prove of great added value both to Enterprise Ireland and to IDA Ireland when they needed to arrange itineraries for visits to DC. The World Bank Irish were always willing to come along and meet Irish visitors to town and often were extremely helpful. I hope that the network survived my departure, but somehow I doubt it.

Recruitment to both institutions was extremely sought after and many got in under the Irish nationality quota (similar to the UN jobs system of national quotas), claiming Irish ancestry. US citizens were especially adept at using this national back door as the US quota was relatively small in comparison to population. We have lots of so-called Irish national staff members whose links to Ireland are tenuous.

Using the World Bank's own official list of Irish staff members, I was amused to come across a Kenyan-born gent who proudly showed me his Irish passport, gained through four years of full-time attendance at the IPA on Lansdowne Road. He, too, had used his Irish nationality status to enter the bank, although as a Kenyan he probably would have received preferential treatment!

One of the little-known schemes surrounding these two institutions is that the Department of Finance and the Central Bank share between them the appointments of the Irish representatives to the most senior board-level jobs which they rotate every two years or so. In my case, it led to a lifelong friendship with Charlie Smith from the Department of Finance and his lovely wife, one of the few which has endured the ravages of a peripatetic career existence. Charlie was without doubt the most helpful of World

Bank contacts and ever ready to make crucial introductions when called upon to do so.

Along with Agriculture, Taxation, Defence, international financial institutions, Congressional lobbying and supervising a major renovation of the Embassy premises, another responsibility I had was as Labour Affairs attaché. I enjoyed this role and it took me into the far reaches of the AFL-CIO, a murky world of wheeling and dealing, with suggestions of organised crime and political influence-peddling. And that was before I watched *The Sopranos*! Trade unionism in the States was tainted by big money and by internecine power-struggles. It was 'interesting', to say the least, that one major politician whom I saw most often at AFL-CIO gatherings was Ted Kennedy. He was close to this US labour movement.

I did have one trusted guide through this quagmire, the late and respected Jim Power. Jim was literally a pipe-smoking legend, a jovial figure with the stature of a friendly Franciscan friar, which he once was. Extremely proud of his Irish roots, he used to tell of his Dad, who served in the notorious Scottish Black Watch regiment, that he had to leave Ireland in a hurry after taking the anti-treaty side in our Civil War. The family was raised in one of the Irish ghettos of New York, the Bronx as I recall, and Jim learned from an early age how to survive and get along with his fellow poor and neglected.

Jim spent many happy years as a Franciscan monk until he discovered sex – and the rest is history. Marrying a fine daughter of the revolution (that is, a descendant of the fighters for independence from Britain), his ever-faithful companion Alice, Jim joined the Federal Conciliation & Resolution Service as a mediator and soon proved to all the value of his religious training.

However, the Irish rebel in him invariably drew Jim, a Kennedy Democrat, to the union side of the argument, and by the time I met him he was under a cloud and out of favour with his Republican-appointed boss. Nevertheless, his survival instincts were skilfully deployed, and we shared many an adventure together that neither the powers (forgive the pun) in Dublin nor DC knew about.

Jim was a Christian, it goes without saying, and a gentle man in every respect, and I missed his reassuring, calm presence in my life on departure from DC. It was a bittersweet moment for me, one of many experienced through the years when leaving behind persons and places I loved.

Another great character I came across in my Washingtonian travels was Dave Aland (still alive and well, as far as I know). Dave persuaded me to join the Annapolis Division of the Ancient Order of Hibernians. Again, I am not exactly sure what he did for a living, a bit of this and a bit of that; he was a member of the NUJ in DC and often entertained me at the National Press Club in DC, a famous landmark. His passion was clearly Ireland and Dave spent most of his waking hours talking, reading and promoting Ireland and all things Irish. He was a one-man Irish Tourist Board. He planned in meticulous detail an annual trip to Ireland with his fellow Hibernians. His pay-off was a free return ticket to Ireland for himself and his delightful wife, Hilda, and board and lodging while acting as guide to the group. Dave spent endless hours squeezing the best deal possible from the already thinly stretched margins of the Irish tourism trade and its operators.

One of Dave's quirks was to mispronounce an Irish place name and to wait to be corrected; his invariable riposte, with a twinkle in his eye, would be to say 'gotcha! The Irish love to correct mispronunciations!' He invented golf stick putters made of Blackthorn wood shafts, a clever notion that didn't quite catch on. That was Dave. But he loved Ireland so much and he knew more about its scenic hotspots than anyone else I know. He was a good friend to all he met and never uttered a cross word, no matter what the provocation. That included some vicious political in-fighting among the AOH membership.

In fact, I was in Washington at a time when Sinn Féin was still outlawed, when an Irish Government Minister would step down from a podium when the 'Shinners' marched by on a St Patrick's Day parade, when there was a concerted effort to denigrate what was seen as extreme 'black-and-white nationalist' organisations such as Noraid. The US State Department, with its fundamental WASP (white Anglo-Saxon Protestant) bias, worked closely both with the UK Embassy and with ourselves on the basis that my enemy's enemy is my friend.

While a feature of the time, Irish foreign policy on Northern Ireland was an inter-island issue on which DFA led, was elitist, anti-nationalist, pro-establishment, with a hint of *mé féin* thrown in for good measure. We favoured the SDLP and accommodation with London over any form of nationalist endeavour.

I chaired some tense Agriculture Attaché meetings in DC during our 1989 EU Presidency (our fourth) as the US, in retaliation for EU non-tariff restrictions on hormone-fed beef, placed a ban on bottled water imports from the EU on foot of a scare that France's Perrier sparkling water might contain carcinogens. In the US, there was a pathological fear of any hint of cancer-inducing substances, whereas in Europe it was all about keeping additives out of food. The French, our predecessors in the Presidency, had made a complete mess of negotiations with the US and it was left to us to calm tempers and find a way forward, which we finally accomplished with a lot of patience and persistence. It struck me at the time that France, for all its self-proclaimed *solidarite communautaire* and protestations of Europe together, was an extremely selfish partner underneath it all, ready to sacrifice any other Member State's interest to save its own. And yet the French are still at the table of 27. No wonder the US doesn't get along so well with their Gallic relatives; 'French fries' says it all.

My first experience of living in the US, on its East Coast, was one I will forever cherish. I got a flavour of the real, normal US, of its short but intense history and patriotic pride. Vacations on the Outer Banks were idyllic; tours of the Civil War battlefields, from Manassas/Bull Run to Harper's Ferry, from Antietam to Gettysburg, were fascinating in bringing the struggle of North versus South alive.

Before we left DC, we flew out west to Arizona to drive from there in a wide loop which took us to the Grand Canyon and Sedona, Monument Valley and the Painted Desert, driving through various Indian reservations along the way, including a memorable stop-over at Window Rock, famous home of the Navajo Tea Company trading station. It was saddening to see the poor state of these reservations with barren soil and sullen groups of idle young men everywhere. Alcohol was not sold on the reservations but that did not stop drink being transported into them by the truckload. And gambling casinos completed the ruination of traditional tribal life. The natural wonders of the red-hued canyons, the mesa rock formations with memories of John Wayne and the cavalry riding to the rescue of stage coaches besieged by Indian hordes, and the wonder of nature in its cactus-filled glory compensated for the depressing reality of life on the range.

In short, it was hard for all of us, adults and children, to say farewell when our time was up. We did go out with a bang though; a little-known deal, whispered in my ear by a former Cunard employee, informed us that a last-minute booking on the QE2 could be had at half price, cheaper than our air-fare entitlements. In those days, the department insisted on single ticketing on the outward and on the return from postings journeys but don't ask me why. So, I have rolls and rolls of negatives with nothing but the North Atlantic to see, as the song says. Oh yes, I do also have one rare shot of the Twin Towers on the Manhattan skyline as we sailed away.

Chapter 5

Dublin and Geneva

Setting Human Rights to right; networking the UN agencies and putting Ireland on their maps; another great Presidency for Ireland; Mary Robinson's African Odyssey; picking up the pieces after her meeting with Robert Mugabe.

HQ, 1990-1993

Returning to the UN & Human Rights Desk in Political Division after four and a half fabulous years at the epicentre of US politics that was 'inside the beltway' in Washington, DC came as a brutal shock for all concerned. In effect, losing good friends we had all made and trying to reignite old friendships was a major challenge. Our son, Barry, then aged 11, pleaded to be sent to boarding school so that he could avoid the pain of making and then losing friends every time we moved.

After an unhappy spell for him at St. Andrews, he was offered a place at Clongowes Wood College in Clane in County Kildare and he thrived there under the loving care of the Jesuit-inspired community. He gave us some immensely proud highlights for the family memories box during his time there, from academic awards through to a decent rugby performance both at Junior and Senior Cup Team level (the late Vinnie Murray was an inspiration to all he coached in Clongowes) and finishing with an impressive tally of points at the Leaving Cert. I hope his son James will appreciate his dad's contribution during his time with the J's and go on to emulate him.

One of his best friends at that time, a couple of years behind him in Clongowes, was David Murphy who, coincidentally, lived a couple of doors up from us on Mapas Road in Dalkey. David was the youngest son of Padraig and Liv Berit Murphy, gifted academically but not a rugby talent. Padraig was a cousin of Paud Murphy whom I had known both in Zambia and again in DC through his trips to the World Bank. More importantly, Padraig was Political Director at HQ, my ultimate new boss, having recently returned from a posting as Ambassador in Moscow. Padraig was a cool customer, seemingly remote and of high intellect, with a droll sense of humour. He was very much in the DFA mould of requiring rigorous attention to detail, pouncing on small errors, but he was generally fair and, as I discovered, he was happy to let those who worked on UN and Human Rights to get on with it.

My first immediate boss in this section was Brendan Lyons, whom I had replaced in DC four years earlier. However, Brendan was already designated to be our first Ambassador in Kuala Lumpur and was soon replaced in the UN & Middle East Section by Sean Whelan, a former colleague from my time in Paris, who was passionate about the Middle East, which was the sexier of the two sides in his bailiwick. I seemed fated to re-encounter figures from my past working life even though I was only 16 years in the department at that stage; perhaps, an indication of just how small the department was for most of the first 75 years of its existence. I often wonder if we truly appreciate how modest the resources devoted to 'external affairs' have been in the Irish Republic?

I recall seemingly endless late afternoon conversations with Sean as he waxed lyrical about the complexities of the Middle East, interspersed with questions to me about Human Rights, combined with solemn debates about whether I should have used a colon instead of an apostrophe and the peril of splitting infinitives. I did learn that the placement of 'both' was often abused, that it should always come before the verb in any comparative clause. 'Capeesh?' as he was fond of saying himself. He was to go on to serve as our Ambassador in Ankara where, sadly, he died of a massive heart attack, I heard, while on the job. Sean lived life well, perhaps too well and far too briefly. *Ar dheis De go raibh an anam, dilis;* you are still fondly remembered and missed.

I found early on that a predecessor, who shall remain nameless but who went on to do great things, had left behind a large pile of unsigned and unratified international human rights agreements. In fact, our record on these was so deplorable at the time that it was rapidly becoming a source of international embarrassment in UN circles. So, my first priority was to tackle the backlog and to improve radically (no split infinitives for me!) our record of adhering to such fundamental texts as the UN Covenant on Civil & Political Rights, on Economic, Social and Cultural Rights, on the Rights of the Child, on Women's Rights and on Freedom from Religious Intolerance, as well as, for example, the Second Optional Protocol of the Abolition of the Death Penalty.

Alas, I was unreasonably, almost hopelessly, optimistic about the timetable for achieving what seemed to me urgent goals in the greater matrix of my tasks. And I had reckoned without Newton's Second Law of Physics (always my worst subject) about every action having an equal and opposite reaction or, in other words, when an irresistible force meets an immovable object, in my case, the formidable physical and intellectual presence of one senior civil servant in the Attorney General's Office.

Inclined to block the progress on any file which crossed his desk, he was determined that Ireland should continue to hide behind various common law pretexts in order to avoid ratifying any international agreements. His real reason for so doing was because it would in most cases require updating and amending our own colonial era laws, anathema to the AGO strategy of the day.

He flatly refused to allow us to proceed to adhere to the Protocol to Abolish the Death Penalty. His reason for doing so was that we might need to invoke that barbarous outdated sanction in the event of the murder of a police officer. It took me a while to overcome this veto, but I finally managed it, with the help of one of Tánaiste Dick Spring's advisors, the looming deadline of a World Conference on Human Rights in June 1993, and with an infinite amount of patience, too, not something I was known hitherto to possess in any great quantity. A government decision outflanked the AG's objections and Ireland became death penalty-free. I felt I had achieved yet another footnote in Irish diplomatic history.

Other achievements I am proud of from this period, apart from a fundamental, vast improvement in our adherence record to international human rights agreements, was to establish a regular and official forum for consultations with Irish NGOs active on Human Rights (for example, Amnesty, Human Rights Watch, the Irish Commission for Justice & Peace) prior to our first UN National Report on Civil & Political Rights.

I had, in fact, the onerous task of editing that report which was extremely well-received by the UN Human Rights Committee in Geneva in 1993, so much so that they recommended it as a template for other countries to follow. And it was interesting that one of the early NGO critics I had to assuage when preparing that report was no less a figure than Rev. (at the time, still under Holy Orders) Michael O'Flaherty, a member of the International Council of Jewish Parliamentarians (ICJP) delegation. No one compared to his commitment to the cause. Michael subsequently joined the UN Human Rights system as an expert, poacher turned gamekeeper.

Council of Human Rights, Geneva, 1990-1997

Apart from the deep personal satisfaction of bringing our deplorable record on ratification of international HR agreements up to a reasonable level and of editing our first National CPR Report, this being Foreign Affairs I was also required to attend the annual five-week sessions of the then UN Human Rights Committee which took place in Geneva during February–March each year. My colleague at the Permanent Mission of Ireland to the United Nations was Colm O'Floinn, a First-Class Honours Graduate from TCD, and it was to be the beginning of a close and constant friendship which lasted through my time in DFA, though our first encounter was not exactly propitious.

The week before I was due to travel out, I got a call from Colm on a Sunday evening to say he had been hitting the ski slopes earlier in the day at a local resort and had fallen badly; a trip to the hospital had shown up a broken leg! It meant that I ended up as his bag-carrier and crutch-minder for the entirety of my first CHR session.

We managed well, regardless. Our New York-based comrade, John Biggar, a keen intellect and a good friend over the years, also joined us for the core debates' period of the sessions and so began an outstanding seven-year run of success in Human Rights promotion and defence for HR Team Ireland. We quickly became known as the Three Irish Musketeers for our advocational adventures, pushing out the boundaries and defending fundamental rights from attack. Among our priority targets were combatting religious intolerance and the death penalty, while promoting the rights of the child and the right to development.

Indeed, the politics of the UN was fascinating to learn from in practice. The structure and the internal dynamics of each of the geographic groups was a wonder to behold, an entire universe largely unknown outside the realms of the practitioners themselves. Not all countries were members of the CHR; that was a matter of election via the UN Economic and Social Council (ECOSOC). There were 54 members who had voting rights and obligations. But to compensate, all countries not elected members were entitled to participate as observers, so the geographic groups took on some importance as spheres of collective influence in how members would vote on certain controversial issues, such as East Timor, abolition of the death penalty, the right to development and so on.

The Western Europe & Others Group, known colloquially as 'Weog', contained the large EU block, usually dominated by a quirky, querulous France whenever they got the chance.

The EU was balanced within Weog by the US, which didn't have a great human rights record in theory ('we apply these rights, not adopt them' was their attitude) almost exclusively interested in picking fights with Cuba and Iran and other rogue states, and to a lesser degree by Canada (women's rights were their preoccupation) and Australia, there to defend Indonesia against our attempts to highlight abuses in East Timor. Surprisingly, a spectacular national lobby campaign by a CIÉ bus driver to mount the East Timor Solidarity Campaign caught the imagination of TDs and thus became a central plank of our HR concerns.

Apart from these former British colonies, the other Weog members hardly counted. The real power struggle was between the EU member states and the US/Canada/Australia. And on American insistence, Israel had been admitted to the Weog sometime previously and was a cipher for US views when they bothered to intervene in internal discussions. They often managed to complicate arriving at a group consensus, especially if any Middle East issue or country were involved, though fortunately Israel didn't have a strong voice within Weog.

I digress; the Eastern Europe geographic group was practically moribund after the fall of the Soviet Union in 1989. Russia and its satellites, Ukraine, Belarus and the 'Stans', worked together but the Baltic republics, Poland and Czechoslovakia didn't participate, preferring to hang around the Weog fringes in what subsequently proved to be a smart move (see Chapter 8).

Africa, the veritable sleeping giant of a group, was by and large led by South Africa, still flexing its post-Apartheid muscles; their Human Rights person was Jack, ironically a white South African. Nigeria kept mum and the North African states occasionally took their own position on issues. CHR Africa Group members often provided the swing votes in any voted resolution. I made it my business to get to know Jack and to persuade him to our cause on occasion. He was a nice guy and I regret that I lost contact with him after leaving Geneva in 1997. I know he was not looking forward to returning to Pretoria where he would be in a small, spurned minority in the South African Department of International Relations and Cooperation.

Latin America was a conundrum of a grouping, enigmatic, hard to herd, disingenuous and contradictory on occasion. Cuba had an overweening, negative, disruptive influence and one could never trust any of the LAC members to vote as they promised. They probably didn't know themselves! They were always pained at having to choose sides, preferring to hide behind consensus and inertia whenever possible. The first UN Commissioner for Human Rights came from Ecuador, which says it all (see below).

The Asia-Pacific group was singularly unhelpful on Human Rights issues. Not only did Indonesia deny any wrongdoing in East Timor, and both India and Pakistan vied for influence and war with one another at the same time, but you had the likes of Iran which ploughed its own angry furrow and most of the ASEAN countries were only interested in economic development issues. Asia-Pacific was always generating complications and potential obstacles to progress on Human Rights.

Such was the international Human Rights landscape when we came to preparations for the World Conference on Human Rights in 1993, the first such conference since the end of the Cold War. Ireland was a prime supporter of the conference within the EU; I saw it as an opportunity to push the concept of a High Commissioner for Human Rights, in similar terms to the existing office of High Commissioner for Refugees, an international public office which had prestige and standing.

Alas, it didn't quite work out that way, although our campaign, which I initiated at working group level in Brussels, was ultimately successful in creating the post. After several tussles with the French in particular, and the Dutch and the British, we managed to get the concept adopted as EU policy. Then Mary Robinson was invited to Strasbourg to chair a preparatory World Conference session of the European region (under Council of Europe auspices) and we convinced the Department of the Taoiseach (the ever affable Brian McCarthy) to let her speak at it. I prepared her brief and Colm prepared her speech. And both of us briefed her orally beforehand on what we were aiming for (an Office of High Commissioner for Human Rights).

She was a great hit with her distinguished diplomatic and parliamentary audience and made a vital contribution in bringing some of the more reluctant members along with us on our journey to the adoption of a High Commissioner for Human Rights at the World Conference in Vienna in June 1993.

And I recall feeling both flattered and humbled when in the Council of Europe reception room afterwards I was singled out by Bride Rosney, Mary Robinson's right and left hand, and the President was brought over to meet me. She began by saying that she had spent the previous 20 minutes chasing me round the room! She then went on to say that she wanted me to know the brief I had done for the occasion was by far the best she had received to date in her Presidency. I took this as a compliment she didn't often hand out. It was the beginning of a close relationship with both women which would endure until 1997.

We took the Strasbourg Declaration and ran with it all the way to Vienna in June. There, we (Colm, John and myself) stormed the bastions of the geographic groups, dividing and conquering each. Amusingly at the time, the US proved to be more parsimonious and less enthusiastic than any other Third Party, which made it much easier for us to convince the Cubans and the Pakistanis that such an office presented no threat in practice. The Latin Americans were bribed by providing its first office-holder, a weak Ecuadorian candidate, Jose Ayala-Lasso.

We knew it would be a massive struggle to get the Office accepted by everyone, that it would be at the expense of a watered-down mandate, but we knew it would be forever – and that someday, someone with dignity and guts would inhabit it to the benefit of all. We didn't dream at the time that that would be our own Mary Robinson!

The Office was officially created by a UN General Assembly resolution in December 1993. I am quite proud and humbled that I took up the idea from a research document, that I pushed it through our own national procedure, through the internecine political intrigues of the EU and, most challenging of all, through the sclerotic, Jabba the Hutt-like bureaucratic stasis that is the UN. It was, I believe, one of the high points of my diplomatic service and a legacy for which I will be happy to share a significant amount of credit.

Other responsibilities took me to regular briefings both at the International Committee of the Red Cross/Crescent (which deals with man-made disasters) and the International Federation (ex-League) of the Red Cross/Crescent which is primarily an umbrella body for national RC organisations whose primary role is to coordinate relief in the case of natural disasters. This role split was confusing for outsiders but seemed to work reasonably well on the ground, with close coordination between the two organisations. Alongside the International Red Cross headquartered in Geneva, one also had the UN Office of the High Commissioner for Refugees and the International Organisation for Migration, which handled the logistics of refugee movements.

Somewhat surprisingly, I discovered while still in Dublin that Ireland had only a simple exchange of letters between our Department of Justice and UNHCR. I set out to improve the basis for our official standing with the UNHCR firstly, by embarrassing Justice into creating a proper legal standing for dealing with refugee status claims; that took a lot of persuasion and time, complicated by our arcane common law system. It helped enormously that my efforts coincided with an exponential leap in refugee claims from a mere handful prior to 1990 to several thousand year-on-year after that date, mainly from the Balkans and the Great Lakes region in Africa.

And secondly, it did not take too much to convince our Development Aid Division (now Irish Aid) to join UNHCR as a full Member, paying an annual fee and contributing to appeals for financial assistance in emergency situations. It seemed odd to me that Ireland had been content with Observer status and had ignored most appeals for help from UNHCR. It helped enormously to have strong support both from within the Division and at the political level in the person of Minister of State, Joan Burton. Joan was extremely active in trying to address the massive emerging tragedy and associated genocidal war crimes that was the Great Lakes crisis on the territories of Burundi, Rwanda and Zaire/Congo.

I like to think that Ireland's aid profile within UNHCR improved hugely as a result of our collective efforts to pursue a more proactive approach and to become more engaged with the organisation at various levels. Certainly, the refugee process in Ireland is now on a more robust and transparent footing though there is still room for improvement, especially when it comes to direct provision as the basis for their reception here.

Move to Permanent Mission of Ireland to the United Nations (PMUN), Geneva

In mid-1993, in what I consider to be a rare moment of lucidity and logic by the Department, I was posted from HQ to Geneva in a direct swap with Colm O'Floinn. I am pleased to say that this worked well for both of us and that Colm completed one piece of unfinished work by successfully lobbying for a dedicated Human Rights Unit, separate from other UN activities such as peacekeeping.

The continuity also enabled me to move seamlessly into his old role in Geneva and, as I have already mentioned, to develop further our bilateral contacts to enhance our profile with other international agencies. So I became familiar with the myriad of humanitarian agencies of various guises, big and small, which inhabited that scenic city by the lake. There was, for example, United Nations University (UNU), UN Volunteers (UNV), Office of the Commissioner for Humanitarian Affairs (OCHA), World Health Organisation (WHO), World Meteorological Organisation (WMO), World Intellectual Property Organisation (WIPO), International Labour Organisation (ILO), UN High Commission for Refugees (UNHCR), UN High Commission for Human Rights (UNHRC), International Council of the Red Cross (ICRC) and the International Federation of the Red Cross (IFRC). If one area went quiet, I simply investigated what was going on in another; there was never a dull moment and I loved the multilateral nature of the work. Michael Noonan, then Minister for Health, visited the WHO and was distinctly unimpressed to be surrounded by doctors who preferred to be well-paid administrators.

Anne Anderson took over from Ambassador John Swift in 1995, and shortly after Anne's arrival I took over as No. 2. Tom Hanney, quiet but with a razor-sharp intellect, joined us on the Disarmament side and together with Pat Fanning and his small team from the Department of Enterprise, Trade and Employment dealing with the WTO, and Brid Canning in the Agriculture portfolio, we faced into the Irish EU Presidency, our fifth, in good shape. Tom went on to have a distinguished diplomatic career, ending up as our Permanent Representative to the European Union in Brussels.

However, our family also had a horrific personal tragedy in the run up to our Presidency in March of that year. It was a Friday afternoon and I was participating in an EU meeting in our rather nice main conference room. My thoughts were turning to a quiet weekend with Siobhán and the children when I got a message asking me to phone home urgently. I went outside to the telephone booth and rang home. A distraught, barely coherent Siobhán told me that she had had a call from Zambia to say her sister, Sandra, had drowned earlier that day at their nursery farm on the outskirts of Lusaka. I am not sure how I got home that day, but I did so in record speed.

Siobhán flew via London with her father and two brothers while I remained in Geneva with our children and went back to Presidency preparations. It was a truly awful period, but we got through it. Sandra's husband Brian and the children joined us for Christmas that year, but it was a very hard time for them all. It is still painful to write about it now.

I do recall one funny incident, though it didn't seem so at the time. In summer 1995, in need of a good summer break before the 1996 Presidency year started, we took advantage of our location to travel south from Geneva, ending up at a seaside resort a little to the east of Marseilles. The apartment we rented was in a gated complex with its own beach access and a large pool so we felt quite secure. I parked our Peugeot 406 car within sight of our particular block, one of several and quite far in from the main road. There was already a Rolls Royce Silver Shadow parked beside our space so I thought that if any thieves did get in, the Roller would be the one they would go for. Wrong!

The following morning, we went for a coastal drive. I noticed on our return to the apartment that there was a small hole directly underneath the driver's door keylock but thought nothing more of it. During the night, which was quite hot so all our windows were wide open, I heard some hushed and 'giggly' voices from what I thought was a nearby apartment.

The next day, Siobhán and myself went out early to get some baguettes and croissants for breakfast. I opened the car as usual and just as I did, Siobhán let out a gasp. The two front seats were missing! I immediately thought of the early hour's disturbance and a student prank came to mind…. I started looking around for the seats! Meanwhile, Siobhán found the tools used to remove the seats. They must have been disturbed as the rear bench was half-way out.

In good Poirot style I picked up the tools and carefully wrapped them in a tea-towel. With the aid of the kind neighbour, he who owned the Rolls and who, it turned out, had a large legal practice in Lyon, we sauntered off to the local police station. A man of influence, my new best friend got us directly to the head of the large queue in front of the Chief Detective's office. I presented the facts and plonked the evidence on his table. He looked down his aquiline nose at me, tore a yellow slip from a pad in front of him and said, 'Give that to your insurance company, Monsieur'.

Flummoxed and flustered, I pointed to the tools from the crime scene. He gestured to me that I could, nay, should take them off his desk and do whatever I wanted with them. I asked him why my seats? He said it was quite common for exotic car parts to be stolen on order by unscrupulous local *garagistes*. My seats had been custom grey leather with an integral heating mechanism, worth approximately the equivalent of 4,000 euros, a good deal more than the car at this stage, which I had bought second-hand from a local garage in Geneva. Obviously, they matched the needs of someone else's auto. Voilà, a regular occurrence during the tourist season on the Cote d'Azur.

The next problem to solve was how to get ourselves and the car home. A visit to a Peugeot dealer (perhaps, the same, who knows!) unearthed a pair of grubby cloth seats of a certain vintage, without seat belts attached – ours had been cut away in the process of stealing the seats. However, to get the car to the garage for fitting the shabby seats, our dealer sent his mechanic with a cardboard box of paint tins. He sat on that and drove our car to his yard.

Arriving home to Geneva sitting perilously on our smelly, second-hand seats, I contacted our insurance company. Fortunately, Swiss law required foreign diplomats to hold first class, fully comprehensive insurance. While the premiums had seemed exorbitant at the time, I now appreciated their true extent. My Peugeot, which I should add had given us great trouble from the start with frequent visits back to where we had bought it, was written off as new replacement custom leather seats would have cost more than the car was worth even before the theft, and I was compensated at full market price of a new equivalent model. I took the money and ran straight to Volvo!

As mentioned, Joan Burton, during her tenure as Minister of State for Development at DFA, was a frequent visitor to Geneva, especially during the Great Lakes tragedy. She impressed with her concern and, of course, her prior African experience as an aid worker in Tanzania helped her in pressing for international action on the genocide taking place, already too little, too late. She resisted attempts by the larger former colonial powers, especially the French, to bully her into acquiescence. I got to know Joan quite well and I believe she trusted my advice when requested. I spent many days and nights tracking the tragedy as it emerged through UNHCR briefings and duly reported back to HQ.

As we now know, France has recently admitted its guilt and the damage it did in its role in that tragedy; one might even describe it as a retrospective apology. Our suspicions at the time of French connivance in these dreadful events have been shown to be all too justified.

In 1994, my path and President Robinson's crossed again. Bride Rosney rang to tell me the president was going on a State visit to Zambia, Zimbabwe and Tanzania; hadn't I been to this part of Africa, she asked? I explained that I had opened the office in Lusaka in 1980 and knew Zimbabwe quite well from frequent R&R visits there. The following day, I received an urgent call from Personnel at HQ asking the same questions and inviting me to volunteer to go to Harare to organise that leg of the three-country State visit. Of course, I jumped at the opportunity.

Within 48 hours, I was on a flight to Harare from Zurich. I landed there the next day and made my way to the UNICEF office which was staffed by an Irish woman who kindly put her modest resources at my disposal. Thus equipped with a phone and desk, I had three weeks to whip a programme together for the President of Ireland. Fortunately, as expected, I found a good network of local Irish, not least among the same Carmelites who had taught me at Terenure College many years previously.

A trip to Protocol at the Zimbabwean Foreign Ministry was an altogether more frustrating affair. While they were aware of the visit, they knew little about Ireland and less about Mary Robinson. Likewise, all arrangements had to be cleared by State House, indeed by President Robert Mugabe himself. That particular megalomaniac was not in a hurry to agree to anything. And, as ever, our local 'Honorary Consul', an elderly gent who displayed decidedly colonial tendencies, wanted to hog the visit for himself, in particular to show Mary off at the annual White Farmer Horse Show.

So I knew from day one that I had my work cut out. However, by summoning previously unknown reserves of patience and testing my diplomatic limits to their utmost, I managed to get a half-way respectable programme agreed on paper. It was the usual mix of State ceremonial activities (such as wreath-laying), relaxation (a game park visit, sight-seeing including a visit to Victoria Falls and private downtime) and educational events (speaking engagement, school and community visit, Irish community gathering). And of course practical logistics, such as a hairdresser on demand, also had to be tied down.

Confident that everything was in place, I flew up to Lusaka the weekend before her arrival to meet the president and her entourage. It also gave me a brief opportunity to meet with my sister-in-law, Sandra, and husband Brian and family. The president got off the plane and on her way into arrivals came over and greeted the Irish who had gathered to meet her, including myself. Bride invited me to join the motorcade and we all went to the Intercontinental Hotel where the Irish party were staying.

I duly checked in with our legendary Chief of Protocol, John Burke, and his deputy, Aidan O'Hara. They professed to be happy with the Zimbabwe arrangements. I warned them that their opposite numbers in Harare were pusillanimous and that arrangements could change abruptly at the whim of Robert Mugabe (I also explained, by the by, with a seriously strained straight face, that the Vice President was, indeed, one Mr. Canaan Banana, but that he was unlikely to appear as he was in bad odour with Mugabe over certain personal habits).

I flew back to Harare that night and was on the tarmac at that skin-tingling moment that our President arrived and the national anthems played for the first time during her visit to Zimbabwe. An airport arrival that included some spectacular dancing and drumming got us off to a fine start. Alas, that was not to endure. The following morning, Protocol switched the timing of the wreath-laying ceremony at the tomb of the unknown rebel soldier with another event. Already our impressive-looking programme booklet was out the proverbial window! A stickler for staying with the minute-by-minute outlined plan, one Irish President let it be known that she wasn't amused. I quickly learned that Mary Robinson doesn't welcome spontaneity.

A trip to the majestic Victoria Falls and to Hwange National Park and Game Reserve, where we literally eye-balled a pride of lions, restored her composure and everyone else's good humour.

The remainder of her visit programme went as scheduled and we were all about to breathe a collective sigh of relief when, with less than 24 hours to go, Mugabe decided he wanted President Robinson to accompany him to his Jesuit boys-only boarding school, two hours' drive north of Harare. Aidan was despatched to check it out in advance and to await her arrival. The two presidents set off in a cavalcade and I gather a trip to the Antarctic would have been warmer. I was left behind in Harare to arrange an early morning departure the following day. I was probably the lucky one!

Returning late that same evening, the President retired directly to her suite. Down in the bar, John B. suggested we 'lash into a glass of red wine' while we had the opportunity to do so as he regaled us with the school encounter. It transpired that President Robinson was visibly fuming while her host showed her off to the assembled pupils and staff. Invited to say a few words, she proceeded to lecture her audience on the deficiencies of single-sex education, especially of the boarding school variety!

Breakfast was a quiet affair, as befitted the solemn mood that had descended on the hotel. A peremptory official thanks was matched by an accelerated departure and truncated airport farewell ceremony. Mugabe stayed in bed.

As I was the designated Irish team sweeper, staying behind to ensure all bills were paid, possessions carried away and no loose ends left, I spent a tense 24 additional hours in Harare, thanking

Protocol without much enthusiasm on either side of the desk. I felt immensely relieved on my own departure back to Geneva; the thought had run through my mind that Mugabe might issue orders for my detention in a fit of spite at the frosty way the visit had ended. He was that kind of dictator and was in total power in Zimbabwe for far too long. His death at 95 went largely unmourned. It had been a country of great potential and actual beauty, but now it lies in ruin.

As my time in Geneva drew to an inevitable close in 1997, our thoughts turned to returning home and to choosing schools for the children. Our eldest, Aisling, she of the one strong hand who once, on a school outing, forced her supervisor to call me to ask if it was all right for her to go mountain biking – of course, was my reply – was in her second last year of the A-level programme and needed one more year in Geneva. HQ were adamant that I could not have the extra year, so we had to send her back to boarding school in Dublin, something we still regret. She did emerge with an excellent Leaving Cert; our Aisling is one determined woman!

This same daughter subsequently showed her strength of character by refusing to accept any adaptation of her driving instructor's car to take account of her lack of a right hand. When it came time to do her test, she similarly refused any special modification or assistance. This caused her to be examined on the test drive by no less a person than the chief examiner for South Dublin, who told her at the end of the test that he 'could find no reason to fail her' and so was obliged to let her through first time!

Out of the blue, one morning in early February 1997, I took a call from Bride Rosney in the Aras. Nothing was said about the 1994 Zimbabwe State visit; I obviously still had some credit in store and memories had faded.

Bride wanted to know what I would think of Mary Robinson making a run for the post of High Commissioner for Human Rights, as Ayala-Lasso's term was up mid-year. I said I thought it would be challenging, that the Office senior staff were known for lacklustre performance and that the Office had a reputation for being something of a dumping-ground for unappreciated UN staff. In addition, the Chinese were difficult Human Rights customers and were muttering about closing the entire operation down.

In other words, I left Bride under no illusion that the role of High Commissioner was a glamorous, powerful one; it certainly was not. But if anyone could turn it round, I was sure our president could with adequate support.

At the following CHR annual session, I discreetly canvassed support for her candidature; rumours and gossip of potential candidates were swirling around the UN coffee bars. I remember I encountered stiff resistance initially from my US colleague, which I thought was a little strange at the time, given our excellent bilateral relations. But as Mary Robinson was herself to discover later on, big countries like the US have interests, not friends.

One of my best contacts in Geneva was Sergio Viera de Mello, originally a brilliant Brazilian diplomat and when I met him a senior official in charge of fundraising in the Office of the UN High Commissioner for Refugees. Sergio was a trusted confidante of the Commissioner, the diminutive but impressive Mrs. Ogata, educated by Irish Sacred Heart nuns in Tokyo. And Sergio was also a trusted emissary of the UN Secretary General Kofi Annan, which meant Sergio had immense influence system-wide; not a man to be crossed.

Shortly thereafter, Mary Robinson's appointment was announced, much to the consternation of the Irish media and general public who, it emerged, were not overly impressed, especially as she was planning to leave her post as president several months prematurely. I received another in a regular series of calls from Bride. This time, the president was looking for my advice on who might be a suitable candidate for the role of Deputy High Commissioner.

I told Bride I could think of no one more qualified in every way, with experience of the intricacies of the arcane UN system and of helping to run a successful agency (the latter an extremely rare quality indeed) than Sergio Viera de Mello. I also knew he was extremely ambitious and would likely consider it as an attractive upward move. I undertook to talk to him.

I phoned Sergio at home on a Saturday morning and we spoke at some length about the opportunity. He subsequently called back on Sunday and said he was interested but would like to go to Dublin and meet the president in person to be sure they would see eye-to-eye. We arranged to travel a couple of weeks later in the margins of some international consultations that we were hosting as Presidency. I picked him up from Buswells where he had been staying, again on a Saturday morning, and I drove him up to the Aras.

I waited outside in the car while he went in with Bride to meet the president. He was back out about 40 minutes later but since he had arranged to meet an old Army colleague outside the gates, we only had a brief chat before he left for the Curragh. He seemed uncharacteristically quiet. I knew from his demeanour that it had not gone particularly well. And so it proved.

Shortly after arriving back in Geneva, Bride rang to say that while the president had been impressed by his experience, she felt that there wasn't a sufficient meeting of minds. Sergio was not impressed by this reaction. But like the professional he was, he brushed himself off, dusted himself down and moved on to new challenges.

Sadly, six years later on 19 August 2003, Sergio was crushed to death in the bombing of the UN HQ in Baghdad, Iraq, along with 20 other members of his staff, where he had been sent as UN Special Representative. Before his death, he was considered a likely candidate to follow Kofi Annan as Secretary General. I always wonder about the twists and turns of fate in this particular case.

Meanwhile, planning for Mary Robinson's arrival moved on apace. Bride was on again about housing and a suitable school. I again set out to find solutions. A trawl of estate agents provided a short-list of potentially suitable rental housing, of which Geneva had an abundance at all price levels.

Bride picked a house convenient to the UN Palais des Nations HQ in a discreet sylvan setting. The house itself was not very large but was well appointed and located, as I said, within walking distance of the UNHCHR offices. It also came within budget; she had now to meet her own accommodation and transport costs, even if well-compensated. It was, of course, quite a change from living with staff at one's beck and call in the Aras gold fish bowl, positively frugal by the standards to which she had grown accustomed, but also a lot more private.

I will say no more about subsequent events; the rest is now history, as they say.

Chapter 6

Interlude in Kildare Street and Onwards to Ottawa

Perseverance, Best Practice and how not to perform at an interview; at the heart of government and cross-border politics; Canadian adventure, short and sweet like an ass's gallop; the Irish contribution to the Rideau Canal; my favourite Aunt Sheila, war bride extraordinaire; UCD in Halifax, Nova Scotia.

A few weeks later, we left Geneva to return to Dublin at the beginning of August. I had assumed my posting home would be a brief one and was not overly concerned to be notified to report to the then-named Department of Enterprise, Trade and Employment. Three weeks' leave helped to settle us into our new house which proved a welcome distraction. I turned up the first week in September to the Department of Enterprise, Trade and Employment in Kildare Street.

The Kildare Street building was an iconic, art deco edifice with an impressive staircase and Connemara-coloured, marbled linoleum throughout. I made my way up to the Trade Division offices where Billy Hawkes was the senior officer on secondment from DFA. I should explain that four years earlier, in 1993, the Fianna Fáil–Labour coalition led by Albert Reynolds decided to shake things up by taking the trade function out of DFA and moving it lock, stock and proverbial barrel, that is, all the DFA Trade Section staff and posts, over to Department of Enterprise, Trade and Employment (or, as it then was, Industry & Commerce, a Ministerial office dear to Albert's heart as a former one, himself). Thus, Billy was the second Principal Officer incumbent, replacing Mary Whelan who had established the DFA bridgehead in Kildare Street.

However, Billy had some surprising news for me. My expectations of being his deputy in the Trade Section were not to be met; that role had been given, in the meantime, to an officer from the Department of Enterprise, Trade and Employment who was transferring home from Brussels. It had been further decided by the powers-that-be in that department (DFA not seeming to be concerned or consulted) that I would be assigned to the Enterprise Division instead. Billy was very nice about it, but I could feel his unease at this development, and it did nothing to quell my own.

I went, as instructed by Billy, up a floor in Kildare Street to the office of Michael O'Donnell, a thoroughly pleasant gentleman of traditional Irish civil service background. I believe I was the first person from DFA to come into direct contact with Michael, and certainly he seemed as puzzled as I was to find ourselves in such close proximity. Michael was kindness itself, and proved to be throughout our three years together. And he was delighted to have an extra body to help with the work of the section, even though I had no idea what I was expected to contribute.

That first week was, indeed, a numbingly terrifying experience, with totally new colleagues in a totally alien environment doing totally unfamiliar work after, at that point, 23 years in DFA. But I knuckled down to it, somewhat consoled by the thought that

I would, any day now, receive the promised call from Geneva to join the new High Commissioner's team there (it never came).

I did go on to fill the role of Secretary to the National Competitiveness Council, an influential position which brought me into contact with wonderful people in the Department (too many to mention but they know who they are) and in the State agencies.

And I was also part of the 'Y2K' team that was put in place to alert the business sector to the potential dangers of out-of-date software which might cease functioning come the advent of 2000 A.D. We toured the country with Minister of State Noel Treacy, a very hard-working Fianna Fáil Deputy, hosting seminars North to South, East to his beloved West, asking companies to check their IT systems and to update them if in doubt. Of course, as we all now know, the dawn of the year 2000 was welcomed by fireworks worldwide and great celebrations but with no evidence of any IT disruption as it did so … a damp squib or a problem over-thought? I maintain that the success of the Y2K campaign globally, including in the Republic, was an indication of the success of such initiatives. And we all know who benefitted.

I worked, for example, hand-in-glove with the remarkable Dr Richard Keegan, a well-known expert on private sector benchmarking tools and on implementing best practice, now known as 'lean'. Together, we managed to get into print a short treatise on benchmarking in the EU as a useful business development tool. Indeed, I enjoyed some amazing trips with Richard to Brussels, Vienna and Helsinki, though not on the back of his Honda Goldwing, I hasten to add. Richard was a bike fanatic, whose notion of a relaxing vacation was to invite his lovely spouse Geraldine into a side car to ride from one end of Europe to the other, hardly pausing to stop and admire the local scenery on the way.

Probably our crowning glory was to bring all six of the state agency chief executives, north and south of the border, together in one place, on the margins of a cross-border seminar on best practice at the Jefferson Smurfit School UCD campus, in February 2001, in order to sign a Joint Memorandum of Understanding on future cooperation in that context.

I believe it was the first such agreement signed by all the agencies together. My role was to assemble all the agency VIPs in the same place at the same time, under the watchful eye of then Tánaiste Mary Harney and her NI counterpart, Reg Empey, shortly thereafter to become First Minister. It proved no small challenge, not least to get our own crowd, Enterprise Ireland and the IDA, to be in the same room at the same time and to sign anything that united them! And it was a first in terms of cross-border economic agreements so another footnote to be proud of.

Mary Harney was an exceptional politician and an impressive Minister and Tánaiste. She had a deep understanding of her brief as Minister for Enterprise and beyond, and could deliver a speech without any prompting or text on the most complex of issues with superb delivery skills and clear knowledge of the subject matter. If the government of the day, or any government for that matter, had been made up entirely of Mary H.-type personalities, our country's future would be in much better shape. And I say that both as a civil servant and as a friend.

Towards the end of my time, a full four-year stint as it proved to be but enjoyable for all that, I was asked to take on the coordination function for a Forfás-instigated OECD review of our national progress towards 'Better Regulation', that is, simpler and more effective regulations and removal of archaic ones. This entailed liaising with various figures in the Department of the Taoiseach and at least one appearance in front of a prestigious OECD Committee when I had to defend some aspects of our far from perfect record to date in relation to the implementation of regulations. It also proved to be a back door into an assault on certain professional services cartels, for example, accountancy, pharmacy, legal practice and the insurance industry.

It was a steep learning curve but a fascinating piece of work, and it stood me in good stead when it came to the next, critical step up the promotion ladder. The year 1999 proved to be an exceptionally bad year for our family: my mum died, my nephew Killian, a twin aged five, was diagnosed with leukaemia and my wife's uncle Mitchel Fleming, who had been in *loco parentis* since she was 14, died suddenly from a stroke. And 2000 was shaping up no better; I had suffered a collapsed right lung, even though I didn't fit the normal medical criteria, being neither tall nor thin.

In February 2000, I threw my hat in the promotion ring in a general, service-wide competition for Principal Officer, encouraged by my experience in the Department of Trade, Enterprise and Employment of the previous four years. I will never forget the interview in a hotel room on Pearse Street. The three-person panel was chaired by an Assistant Secretary in the Department of Social Welfare. It was scheduled for 9.00 am; I was the first one in before them that morning. After an hour's delay, during which sweaty palms were displaced by mental panics of one kind or another, totally destroying my preparation and concentration, I was eventually called in. A short apology was offered by the chairman who said he had been delayed. He then started off asking me to tell them what I had been doing for the previous 26 years. At the end of the interview, he looked me straight in the eye and said, 'Thank you for a tour of the world,' and that was that.

A week later, DFA held an internal promotion competition. I had had feedback from the PO competition that I was too solemn, too serious at interview so I went in with a smile bursting from ear to ear and joked that if I was smiling like the Joker in *Batman*, it was because I had been told I was too serious at interview – and, to my amazement, it worked!

I heard afterwards that the Board had wanted to give a chance to people like myself who had served our time to the best of our ability and who were both experienced and still motivated despite the long wait which, by the way, was a direct result of the 1974 recruitment bulge. I also heard back that my regaling of four years' experience in Department of Enterprise and Employment had also come across well.

Whatever their motivations, I am eternally grateful for the opportunity to advance that they provided and I believe I have lived up to their expectations and confidence in me. Since that crucial promotion, I went on to be a proactive Consul General in the western US, from there to open a new Irish Embassy in Lithuania, to play a key role in our most recent EU Presidency and to explore new frontiers as Ambassador to Finland.

When one hears that the average age on promotion to Assistant Secretary General rank these days is 42, I feel I did rather well to get any at 50!

Ottawa, 2001

However, before that news came through, I had departed a week earlier on what was to be the shortest, but also one of the sweetest, of my postings, Ottawa, saying a fond farewell to the lovely group of friends and colleagues I had made during my time in Kildare Street.

Prior to my official arrival in Canada, I had accepted with alacrity an opportunity to spend a week in Ottawa over St. Patrick's Day, when Minister Mary Hanafin and her spouse Eamon Leahy would be visiting. I was also excited at the prospect of seeing my Aunt Sheila, my late father's sister. Their mother, Mary, née Murtagh, had died quite suddenly in 1943, leaving behind five children in their teens to sustain themselves (Grandad Denham had passed away in 1935). Sheila took the emigrant route to England, finding herself a job as a dental receptionist in North Yorkshire.

I heard only recently that dentists were in high demand during the war, that dental problems among bomber crews were exacerbated by flying – rotten teeth exploding not uncommon – so it wasn't surprising to hear she had met my Uncle Charlie Gaulin in the waiting room. He was a mechanic with the Royal Canadian Airforce bomber squadron located nearby the practice. They were married shortly after the war ended at the Church of The Three Patrons in Rathgar, near the modest Denham family home on Garville Road. Uncle Charlie had the distinction of being married in his splendid air force uniform, an unusual sight which caught the attentions of Dublin newspapers, I gather.

Charlie was posted home shortly afterwards but Aunt Sheila had to wait a further twelve months before the Government of Canada got around to organising a ship to transport some 300 British and Irish war brides who had been impatiently waiting to join their spouses. The ship sailed from Liverpool and Sheila recounted that for four of the five days' passage across the Atlantic all of the women were violently seasick, such was the discomfort of their transport. They finally docked in Halifax, Nova Scotia, at Pier 21, which is now one of the most-visited tourist attractions in Canada. I had the pleasure of buying a plaque with Sheila's name on it, mounted on one of the Pier shed walls.

By early 2001, I was ready to leave Dublin again after what was a long and challenging home assignment, what we unkindly refer to in DFA as 'the real hardship post'. Living abroad for four years has its own complexities; living overseas is quite unlike being a tourist. One experiences the same pains and pleasures as do the locals. We work, travel, shop and eat as local people do. A different language adds a further dimension. We do not spend our free time visiting tourist attractions and eating our way through mountains of Ferrero Rochers.

But we are reasonably well paid when abroad – although Ireland is well down the comparative international scale of diplomatic allowances and other perks. And we do feel special, and proud to be Irish when away en poste, which is not always the case back home. So, for me, a foreign posting has always been preferable to a home-based one.

Canada was a country I had always thought would be interesting to serve in, with a rich tapestry of history and diverse culture. Both Francophone and Anglophone, in geographic terms it is the second largest in the world after Russia. And, as I was to learn, it was very conscious of its position to the north of the United States. I was told early on that 90 per cent of the population of Canada lived within 100 kilometres of the US border.

For all that, arriving in Ottawa via Boston in 2001 – there were no longer direct flights to Canada which surprised me – felt distinctive and reassuring. Ottawa Airport was quite small and dominated by Air Canada's maple leaf logo. A short journey took me to what I was told was the leafy suburb of Rockcliffe, to a ginormous house which we had bought for a good price back in the 1950s. It had a slightly unfinished feel, with a beautiful entrance and superb, recently refurbished dining room, but rather bitty reception rooms and distinctly dated bedrooms, including a large, boarded attic space over the garage. However, the leaves were not in evidence; instead there were two to three feet of snow which was replenished by Mother Nature almost every day.

The official car which was kept at the house was a seven-year old Volvo, an unfortunate deep green colour. My mother once told me that green cars were 'unlucky' and, indeed, there may be something in that old wives' tale as most people who are colour blind are green-blind. I was fascinated to learn that with normal sub-zero daily temperatures, the car had to be plugged into a heater every night to stop it from seizing up. It was obviously important to unplug it every morning before driving away!

Ottawa has a bit of pomp and ceremony that the US lacks. The Governor-Generals live in a fine mansion with sentries in Busby and red tunic, a guard-changing ceremony to rival Horseguards Parade in London, and a fine parliament building in high Victorian style that could put the mother of parliaments at Westminster to shame. Royal Canadian Mounted Police (RCMP), also known as the Mounties, on horseback in their red and black uniforms and pointy hats complete the picture of a country that holds on to its fine traditions. The Mounties' stables were close to the house in Rockcliffe and a frequently visited spot by visitors to Ottawa.

I also tried to get in a visit or two outside of the capital whenever opportunities presented. In my view far too many diplomats, especially Heads of Mission, tend to sit in their palatial offices and can't be bothered to travel extensively for the duration of their postings. Such colleagues do the rest of us a great disservice.

One of my first trips was to Swift Current, Saskatchewan, at the invitation of the Provincial Chamber of Commerce, to address their AGM on the 'success story' that was the Irish economy of the time (those were the days!). A quick look at my map of Canada indicated that Swift Current was a fairly modest-sized town about 200 kilometres west of the provincial capital, Regina (so-named after Queen Victoria in whose reign the territory was settled). Neither place looked too far away on the map.

However, the flight from Ottawa to Regina took the best part of five hours, the equivalent of London to Moscow. Regina itself proved to be a sweet little place, a rail stop on the great continental track linking Eastern Canada with Vancouver in the West, via the great plains and prairies of Manitoba, Saskatchewan and Alberta, the historic pioneer trail of yore, built largely by Irish and Chinese labour navvies in the mid-nineteenth century. Trains using this route now were mostly cargo runs only, but the engines still retained those wonderful steam-horn toots, jingle bells and clanking wagon sounds made famous by Hollywood Westerns!

I took the opportunity in advance to contact the small Irish Society of Regina and invite them for a meet and greet reception. And I am so glad I did. I met a group of the nicest people you could come across, delighted to meet 'their Ambassador'. It turned out to be the first such occasion in living memory that anyone from the Irish Embassy in Canada had visited Regina.

The following day, I rented a car and headed west in the direction of Swift Current – 199 kilometres later I was still driving in a completely straight line along a seemingly never-ending road, deserted in both directions, and with shimmering, billiard-table flat salt pans for as far as the eye could see. It was, as I then realised, exactly as I had been told by my Regina Irish friends: 'You can let your dog off the lead … and still see them two days later!'

My welcome at Swift Current couldn't have been warmer; it was as if Amundsen had arrived back from the North Pole! I was a local celebrity, treated to the best room in the hotel, modest though it was, and wined and dined accordingly. I was interviewed both for the local TV station and by a print journalist, and I have to say they were very decent in their coverage, highlighting the great friendship between our two countries.

At one stage, I asked naively what was the largest big town near Swift Current (I was always fascinated by locational geography). I was told with a wry smile that the nearest conurbation to Swift Current, Saskatchewan, was a little place about 200 kilometres directly southeast, across a lake, by the name of Chicago. I think they may have been joking because Swift Current is nowhere near Chicago on any map I have since looked at.

Montreal in Quebec was another place I visited on several occasions, taking a comfortable train ride to get there. A wonderful Irish Canadian community welcomed me, especially a lady named Elizabeth Quinlan and her friends. Our Honorary Consul there was, by contrast to most, quite professional in his approach. His then counterpart in Toronto, Ted, was a most pleasant, easy-going semi-retired banker who was of great assistance whenever I visited that city; such are the vagaries of the Honorary Consulship system worldwide.

Montreal has a place near and dear to my heart. It was shortly after checking into a rather depressing, brown décor hotel room in downtown Montreal, where I was to be the guest of honour of the Montreal Irish Society on the Friday before 17 March 2001, that I got an email offering me the promotion to Counsellor level, after 26 years of waiting, hoping and never giving up. That night's celebration was among the best of my life! I can still feel the glow of happiness!

Mary Hanafin, Minister of State for Children in the Fianna Fáil–Progressive Democrats coalition, who was pleasant to work with and rigorous in application to her brief, and her spouse, Eamonn Leahy, Senior Counsel, were our government visitors for the main Canadian St. Patrick's Day celebrations in Ottawa and Toronto that year. The Toronto Irish Society had a men-only lunch for over 1,000 which Mary addressed; she was masterful, winning over her audience with some witty opening remarks and receiving a standing ovation. That night, Eamonn, one of the nicest gents on God's earth, took us out to dinner. He was a noted oenophile and treated us to some really special vintages. Eamonn was also a wonderful raconteur and regaled us with delightful tales of his courtroom encounters in prosecuting some of the most dangerous criminals in our society, though he was modest about it. Shortly before the Canadian trip, he had helped put away John Gilligan, a fascinating episode in the recounting.

Alas, it was with deep sadness that I learnt of his sudden death in 2003. I still can only guess at the pain and loss. May he rest in peace.

We also were on the reviewing stand for the St. Patrick's Day Parade in Toronto, an impressive affair, not on the scale of New York but significant nonetheless. It was with some disappointment that the Minister was not greeted by Mrs. Galen Weston, previously Mary Frayne, Dun Laoghaire-born and then Lieutenant Governor of Ontario.

But I did meet Gordon Morrison and his lovely, Limerick-born wife Marie O'Shea, then the Desk Officer for Ireland at the Canadian Foreign Ministry HQ in Ottawa. The Ministry's iconic building, named after Lester B. Pearson, one of Canada's most famous pre-war premiers who also held the Foreign Affairs portfolio, is situated beside the Rideau River. In summer Marie, also a diplomat, and Gordon, who together lived two miles upstream, would canoe to work. In winter, they used snowshoes to travel along the deep frozen waters of the river. A photo feature of their unique commute appeared in *The Ottawa Journal.*

It was from conversations with Gordon that I was able to convince both Dublin and Ottawa to resuscitate a long-dormant Student Summer Work Visa programme, accelerating numbers from 50 to 500 initially, to over 1,000 within a few short years. There is now a fully-fledged two-year Work Visa Programme in place through the follow-up efforts of colleagues at the Embassy.

Gordon, who was from Liverpool, Nova Scotia, a small fishing port south of the provincial capital of Halifax, also put me in touch with the Irish Society of Nova Scotia, and an invite to speak to them followed which was accepted with alacrity.

The welcome hospitality shown throughout my two visits to Halifax was provided by Helen Ferguson and her spouse, Lorne, a lovely couple with whom we became the best of friends. Helen worked for the State Department of Tourism & Cultural Promotion and was an ardent fan of folk traditions with a particular fondness for Irish music and its contribution to Canadian folk heritage. As a result, Ireland has a wonderful, active local society which punches way above its weight.

Halifax has one of the world's deepest and largest natural harbour anchorages and was used extensively during World War II to assemble convoys therein prior to setting out across the treacherous North Atlantic.

It is also the location of what residents claim is the oldest Irish third-level educational institution outside of Ireland, St. Mary's University, founded as a school for boys by Bishop John Burke in 1802, and later developed into a university first by Irish Christian Brothers and latterly by Irish Jesuits. While in Halifax I was invited by Cyril Byrne, a professor at SMU, who had been running an Irish Studies programme for some time there, a lonely furrow to plough by all accounts, with little external support.

Cyril, a slightly portly gent with a twinkle in his eye and a distinctive Irish accent from somewhere in south Dublin, gave me a warm welcome; the main building was not a million miles in its façade from UCC's portico. We had been talking for about thirty minutes, most of that time taken up by Cyril talking and me listening, when I noticed the tie he was wearing was covered in harps. Naturally curious, I asked him where it was from?

'Do you not know a UCD tie when you see one?'

'No, of course not, I'm a Trinity guy.'

'Ah,' says Cyril.

So, encouraged by my winning streak so far, I ventured, 'And what part of South County Dublin is your accent from?'

'St. John's Newfoundland!' replies the bold Cyril, quick as a wink! Touché!

We became firm friends after that, and I came back a few months later to spend a brief week's holiday in his company and that of his partner, Laurie. Laurie was from Peggy's Cove, site of a famous lighthouse, and her brother was still living there as a renowned woodworker. He specialised in making bodhrans, believe it or not, and I commissioned a fine specimen from him which hangs on a wall of our home. One of my bucket list projects is to learn how to play it. We travelled extensively and Cyril showed off the fascinating historic locations across the province.

At one point on a beach at Lunenburg, one of the prettiest of Nova Scotia's old fishing ports, I made the mistake, on a very hot day, of dipping my toes into the water's edge. The shock of cold was instantaneous! I had forgotten that our side of the Atlantic is warmed by the Gulf Stream while Canada's is cooled by icebergs! If ever there was a hard-won lesson it was that moment.

Cyril and myself planned to take a ferry across from Sydney, Nova Scotia on the Cape Breton coast to near Cape Ray, Newfoundland to explore the French and Irish roots of his ancestral home. The Byrnes were one of a large number of Irish families from Waterford who, beginning in the eighteenth century, had used Newfoundland as a summer base from which to fish the Grand Banks off the coast.

As time progressed, more and more of the fisherfolk stayed on throughout the year and so Newfoundland became colonised, on its East Coast, from Ireland. The west and south of Newfoundland remained under French colonial influence and St. Pierre and Miquelon remains to this day a Territoire D'outre Mer of the French Republic. It was my greatest wish to make that trip with Cyril – we shared a love of boats and of sea journeys, especially adventurous ones – but it was not to be.

I was subsequently despatched after my brief sojourn in Canada to the US West Coast and while I remained in occasional touch with Cyril in the years that followed, it was with great sadness that I learnt that he had been diagnosed with a vicious and fast-growing cancer which took him from us far too young. So many good people have been in and out of my life for such a short period.

Halifax itself was one of my favourite places to visit. The port area has a small glass factory down at the Quay wall which makes crystal glass that rivalled the best of that of Waterford Crystal; and why not, since it had been founded by former glass blowers from Waterford made redundant when the company went into terminal decline in the late 1980s.

As I mentioned at the beginning of this chapter, further along the harbour is Pier 21 which had become one of Canada's most-visited tourist attractions. Pier 21 is the historic site of twentieth century sea-borne immigration to Canada from Europe. Hundreds of thousands of immigrants landed at Pier 21 before and after World War II before being sent by train all across this vast country. Among them was my Aunt Sheila, war bride, who passed through on her way to be reunited with Uncle Charlie in 1946, though she had to wait a year as other priorities prevailed at the time.

When I met her many years later in Ottawa, Aunt Sheila was in her eighties, but was still one feisty woman with that great determination that her generation seemed to possess in spades. She still walked a mile every day for exercise and got up on the garage roof in winter time to shovel off the snow drifts! Her only concern was that since she had reached the age of eighty, the authorities would take her driving licence away one of these days. She dreaded the yearly tests to which she was subjected yet always passed them with flying colours. Imagine the things we worry about!

My fifty-first birthday party was celebrated under the stars in the embassy garden at Rockcliffe Park; we moved a table out for the occasion and had a wonderful meal during which more than one Canadian guest amazed me with renditions of what

With Bono and Daithi O'Longaigh in Portland.

The author, President McAleese, Siobhán, Martin in Seattle.

The Vilnius skyline.

My Vilnius, in front of Gedimino.

Professor Dovid Katz, brilliant scholar and a good friend.

Credentials ceremony, Vilnius, 2005, with President Valdas Adamkus
and our son Barry as special guest; a proud family occasion.

Эта дорога ведет к братской могиле,
где в 1942 году зверски убиты
немецко-фашистскими захватчиками
600 еврейских детей и 200 стариков -
жителей Ивенца и окрестных деревень

Site of Holocaust massacre just outside Minsk.

Fania Brankovsky, Holocaust survivor, World War II heroine,
guerilla fighter, a truly remarkable person.

1962 era ICBM silo in deepest Lithuania.

Credential presentation, Minsk, with Europe's 'last dictator',
President Alexander Lukashenko.

With Adi Roche outside an Irish aid clinic under construction, Belarus.

Welcome to Russia! On the Finnish-Russian border.

Handover of the Finnish translation of the Irish Proclamation, Turku, June 2015.

Andrea, Didi, Barry and Aisling say goodbye to Finland.

are formally termed 'dramatic monologues', seemingly endless stories in verse. One example of this popular early twentieth century art form is *The Green Eye of the Little Yellow God* by J. Milton Hayes with its famous character, Mad Carew. We had such good, civilised fun that night. We parted as the dawn was breaking through and the Arctic stars receded. I suppose that is why I liked Canada so much. It was civilised yet simple, an outdoors existence free from fear and terror. I should like to have been born a Canadian.

My other claim to fame in this short period in Canada was to be in the right place when the Irish Society of Kingston, Ontario, decided to commemorate those many unsung heroes who built the Rideau Canal, linking Ottawa with the Great Lakes system at Kingston. They were communities of workers recruited by Lord Monck from his estates in Northern Ireland in the 1820s who, after surviving the perils of the crossing to Canada, took on a tough and equally dangerous challenge in hewing out a channel through hard rock and forest.

The canal and its many locks along the way were built between 1828 and 1832. In doing so, many perished, either from accident or disease – cholera and typhus were prevalent among both workers and their itinerant families – and their remains were deposited in unmarked graves along the way. The Kingston Irish Society organised plaques to mark these graveyards and the Embassy, through support from our cultural funds was able to make a financial contribution to make this possible. My name is on one of the memorial plaques which is placed at Chaffey's Lock, one of the most notorious of the grave sites.

Among the more interesting EU Heads of Mission monthly meetings which I attended in Ottawa involved the Head of

Hydro Quebec, a Canadian mega power generation company. He explained quite calmly that most electric power was generated on the eastern seaboard but that instead of being transmitted to western Canada, where major energy-thirsty industries, especially lumber, were located, Canadian supplies were being sent south of the border to be gobbled up by the city of New York. The Big Apple was then almost totally dependent on Canada for its voracious power consumption. Our guest went on to say that the New York grid was so old and so rickety, having been added to haphazardly over the years of rapid growth without any thought being given to long-term consequences, that it was then, in 2001, on the verge of collapse. Brownouts would give way to blackouts as the city power supply struggled to meet demand. He was not too sanguine about the long-term future of that great city ... and that was well before the Trump era!

All too quickly it seemed, the Department notified me of my next posting, on promotion, as Consul General to the Western United States, based in San Francisco. My replacement in Ottawa was to be Martin Burke with whom I had served in Washington, DC back in the 1980s. Increasingly, as I have said already, it appeared that paths cross and recross in our small diplomatic service. Martin expended a lot of energy on Anglo-Irish affairs during his time in DC and earlier, for which he was rewarded with the post of Ambassador to Australia. Martin subsequently served in Stockholm, Ottawa and finally Berne, retiring after a continuous run abroad of several decades.

I flew home with great sadness in my heart at leaving Canada – and my Aunt Sheila – behind, on 10 September 2001. The following morning, though I didn't know it, I was waking up to a brave new, forever changed, world.

Chapter 7

San Francisco and the West Coast

The western edge of Empire, two million square miles, 13 states (almost) in four years; the Irish in the West and the Irish in the East, never the twain shall meet; encounter with Colin Farrell, how he ended up on crutches, expletives deleted; Bono and others; Brian Cowen, 'never bullshit a bullshitter!'

I arrived home from Ottawa on 10 September 2001. I was fairly jetlagged after a hectic departure schedule and so was up quite late on the following day. My daughter Andrea was at home, on sick leave from school. As usual, she was plonked in front of the telly. A casual glance told me she was watching some old US movie, perhaps, *Inferno*. 'Dad, Dad,' she screamed, 'Come here quick and watch this.' It was CNN and the second aeroplane was just literally crashing into the side of the World Trade Center building. The rest, as we know, is one of those epic moments in history, along with the JFK and RFK assassinations, which I have lived through.

My first instinct was to call the department and offer my services. These were gratefully accepted by Assistant Secretary Margaret Hennessy who was in charge of Human Resources at the time. I spent the next 48 hours in Iveagh House helping to set up a help-line service for those concerned about relatives and friends in New York, and liaising with our Consulate and elsewhere trying to establish a list of those caught up in the awful tragedy. It was harrowing work, but we eventually got a reasonably accurate list of names of those injured or dead which we used in responding to calls from the public. It was a traumatic experience but obviously worthwhile; the operation was very much made up on the hop.

But the department did learn a valuable set of lessons from it and, as a result, was much better prepared for future catastrophes. It now has a permanent standby emergency response team and procedures which click into operation once a disaster has occurred. Thus, for example, the Southeast Asian tsunami and the Japanese nuclear earthquake incidents saw the department better prepared than some of its nearest neighbours.

So it was after a few weeks further delay that we set off for that great City by the Bay. Our initial arrival on Aer Lingus in Los Angeles (there were no direct flights to San Francisco) brought home to us the forever-changed brave new world that travellers now lived in post-9/11. Not only did we have third degree searches both in Dublin and on transfer in LA, but we were both singled out for a final 'random security search' just before stepping on to our connecting flight to San Francisco. As we were to discover, this became a regular occurrence on domestic flights over the next twelve months. It seemed our Irish passports which we were obliged to show at check-in were enough to trigger the so-called pre-boarding 'random security check' which 'foreigners' had to endure in travelling in US airspace. While we had no problem in complying, it did make a bit of a nonsense of the random approach to homeland security. It also brought back memories of the bad ol' days ten years earlier in DC when IRA bombings tarred us all with the terrorist brush.

San Francisco was like dying and going straight to heaven. What a glorious piece of global real estate! We really couldn't believe how every single day was as good as, if not better than, the one that went before. 'Flowers in our hair time, little cable cars reaching halfway to the stars!' And I had, as Consul General, a remit of two million square miles to cover, 13 western states; sure, one need never be bored! I also had the great good fortune to have a Third Secretary quite unlike any other and completely competent and in tune with my own thinking, the Mary Poppins of DFA, Fiona Hunt, and her able companion and spouse, Jimmy Penollar. What a team we all made!

Mind you, I did find the open gayness of the society a bit disconcerting at first; it was very much in your face. But after a while, one adjusted and the whole issue faded into the background. What never faded was the large number of homeless on the streets of this magnificent city, some 14,000 (yes, thousand) of them, wandering around, begging, sleeping in doorways and alleys, harmless to everyone except themselves.

One of my early encounters was with St. Anthony's Dining Room, a downtown centre run by the Franciscans feeding lunch to several thousand homeless people 365 days a year. It really was quite moving, Christ at work in the most practical way. St. Anthony's had also developed into providing other social services such as temporary accommodation and employment through a farm they ran just north of the city. I became one of the many volunteers in the Dining Room and found it the most inspiring experience of my time in San Francisco. Each volunteer ate the same food and sat with the Dining Room patrons. Many of them were armed forces veterans and had served in Vietnam; they had been abandoned and forced on to the streets by closures of residential facilities under Ronald Reagan.

St. Anthony's had a rule that it would never accept any state or federal aid, nor would it invest in any long-term revenue sources. This meant that their annual budget started at zero every 1 January and that they spent everything they received in the calendar year. The miracle was that every year, St. Anthony's would be accepting donations from individual donors and, especially coming up to Christmas, large cars would pull up outside and disgorge well-heeled people of all ages with donations at the ready. It was quite a spectacle; God providing sufficient needs to these unfortunate people every year.

The only wrinkle with living on the West Coast was that its location meant it was on a different time zone from the East Coast, for example, which meant that the Consulate was always half a day behind Dublin. Mind you, Fiona and I quickly worked out that an early, Starbucks -fuelled start meant that we had caught up by lunchtime, that Dublin was winding down by then and that long lunches spent dissecting both local and national political issues were most agreeable. This was followed by yet another intensive burst in the early afternoon which would see us ahead of HQ again, which meant an on-time finish and often, if no after-hours functions loomed, a round of golf on one of the local public courses or an inspection tour of the Irish pub scene in the misnamed Sunset district.

I recall that we counted over forty such establishments there, ranging across the spectrum from shebeen to elegant dining, each with its own distinctive and loyal clientele. In fact, there was even a traditional patronage pattern based on which were early pubs to visit on a Friday evening to those which went on well into the night. It was possible to track down certain people we might be looking to speak to once we knew these individual bar proclivities.

Our immediate priority was to find a place to live at a rent we could afford. I enjoyed the search and it helped in learning our way around what is a compact major city by US standards, a mere 45 square kilometres of peninsula poking into the most spectacular bay in the world, without a doubt. Choices, choices, we finally settled upon a charming duplex apartment in an old building on Hyde Street, overlooking the famous cable car terminus of the same name. While it didn't quite match commuting to work by canoe or snowshoes mentioned in the previous chapter, travelling daily by 100-year-old cable car to the office must rank as one of the more exotic means possible! I certainly enjoyed doing so on an occasional basis, but quickly discovered the walking short-cuts which I found so interesting to follow in that treasure of a city. Mind you, the 'F Market' trolley-type streetcar service, which used old stock from the 1940s gathered and preserved from what was once a vast network of iconic US urban transport systems, was also a joy both to behold and to experience, and I recommend a trip from Market Street to the Fisherman's Wharf terminus.

One of my first tasks was to find new premises for the Consulate as our lease was due to expire shortly after my arrival, and the building was to undergo an extensive renovation which would necessitate removing all the tenants for an extended period as well as a hefty rent increase. The space, which we had occupied for a long number of years, had also grown far too small for our needs so there was no choice but to go hunting for a new location.

Again, I quite enjoyed the experience of looking at what was available. It allowed me to explore the downtown surroundings and we even got a chance to look at rental space inside the Transamerica Pyramid, the second tallest building which branded the skyline of the City by the Bay. Alas, the price per square foot was way above our modest budget but it was worth seeing the view from the tower.

After a considerable amount of time and effort, and some near-miss negotiations, Fiona and I finally found 100 Pine Street, 33rd floor, not by any means the tallest of its kind in San Francisco but with spectacular views of the Golden Gate and the North Bay on one side and Oakland and the Bay Bridge on the other. So it was that both at home and at work, I had the most stunningly visual environment; it has never been equalled since.

With that sorted, I undertook a programme of visits to Irish communities across the consular area. Thus I visited Barney, our Honorary Consul in Reno, Nevada. Why, one may ask, does Ireland have an Honorary Consulate there when we didn't have one at the time in Las Vegas, never mind San Diego or Seattle? The file revealed that Barney, a pleasant, almost diffident individual with a good wife, Marge, behind him, was a doctor who had emigrated from Donegal a considerable time before to take up a teaching appointment at the University of Nevada-Reno. A sustained letter-writing campaign to be awarded the title of Honorary Consul, with letters to Irish politicians of every persuasion, had eventually overcome the inherent objections of a succession of Irish Ambassadors in DC and Consulate Generals in San Francisco, all of whom questioned the priority and supposed added value in making such an appointment. To be fair to him, Barney took it seriously, creating a small but colourful consular office space in his delightful desert home. If anyone had ever wandered close and had needed consular assistance, they would have been well-treated by our said Hon. Con. Alas, virtually no one did, for the Irish of Nevada, rather small in number, resided for the most part in the glorified gambling den that is Las Vegas.

My travels also took me quite often both to San Diego where I had great help from Rob Mullaly, an Irish émigré from Jamaica, and to Seattle, where John Keane from Galway was doing an absolutely excellent job, in retirement, of promoting links with Ireland and providing practical help to the occasional consular case which passed through this large west coast city.

Not quite as spectacular a seaside location as its southern sister, San Francisco, Seattle nonetheless had a fine downtown and a thriving Irish community. I had heard stories of the lousy climate, a city permanently enveloped in rainstorms blown in from the northern Pacific, but I never actually experienced more than an occasional shower in any of my frequent visits. In fact, during Mary McAleese's official visit there in May 2005, the sun split the stones with record highs in the eighties which got me into trouble for being overly pessimistic in my pre-visit notes. Pike Street Market was a nice place to visit in Seattle and the Irish community there was always most welcoming.

For me, Seattle has a fine university community and with both Boeing and Microsoft, never mind Starbucks, it presents a comfortable 'academic air' of intellectual pursuit as well as of earnest innovative endeavour in a studious European rather than brash West Coast American flavour. Riddle that!

I asked Fiona to go to Salt Lake City for the 2002 Winter Olympics and she came back raving about the wonderful welcome she had received from the Irish community there, at the epicentre of the Made in the USA Mormon religious movement, also knowns as the Church of Jesus Christ of Latter-day Saints founded by Joseph Smith and Brigham Young. The latter rather eclipsed Joe Smith and his brother and putative successor, Hyrum, both of whom were killed by a mob in Illinois.

The eponymous Brigham (he has both a town and a university called after him) led his people, Moses-like, out of the Illinois swamps and to the promised desert land of Utah in the mid-1800s, and having clashed with a US federal army in skirmishes in 1858, managed to assert a totalitarian grip on the fast-growing city by the salt lake. His penchant for polygamy, 'I have a burning in my bosom for another wife' (totalling 29 before he had finished burning himself), gave him notoriety but the church has since become a pillar of respectable, conservative society and is known for its famous Mormon Boys Choir and its vast collection of accessible genealogical records. The Church HQ dominates Salt Lake City and is fascinating to tour. The large number of young people in black strolling around it is striking, as they prepare to 'go on mission'. The Mormon faith now numbers over 15 million world-wide, half in the States and Mexico and the remainder largely in Central and South America; I found them interesting but rather nebulous to engage with in conversation.

Whereas the Irish community is typically on for anything, in Utah the strait-laced Mormon environment encouraged them to act accordingly! One such example was a trip they organised for me to Promontory Point, Ogden, Utah, site of a unique US National Park visitors centre, where two old Wild West-style locomotives puff towards one another every day along a short stretch of track, screeching to a halt, cow-catcher to cow-catcher, and blowing off copious amounts of steam and high-pitched whistles with musical tinkling bells thrown in, reminiscent of John Wayne movies. They must have known of my fascination for trains.

We met the park director, a pleasant woman who showed us around and even let us climb aboard one of the engines. The reason for the park and for the daily engines ceremony, she explained, was to commemorate the meeting point of the Union Pacific and the Central Pacific railroads in the first major transcontinental US land connection of over 3,100 kilometres in 1869. The 'last spike' (made of gold) was driven in at a special ceremony at Promontory Point and recorded for posterity in a famous early photo, carried in newspapers around the world. The Union Pacific navvies were predominantly Irish; they built east to west from Ohio, across the Great Plains. The Central Pacific workers were mainly Chinese labourers. Especially imported for the hazardous task, they had the shorter but far more arduous and lethally dangerous task of blasting and digging their way over and through the mighty Rocky Mountain route. For them, the meeting in Ogden was a walk in the park, an anti-climax after what they had come across.

I thanked the director for her kind welcome but expressed some disappointment on hearing that the exact location of Promontory Point was in fact several kilometres further northwest, sealed off from access in the desert foothills, and that the original 'iron horse' track had long been ripped up, during World War II to be exact, and the rails used for weapons manufacturing.

No special pleading would sway her into letting us visit the site which the park service wished to keep undisturbed.

A wink from one of my Irish community companions announced that there was something afoot about which I should stay strum. We took our departure from the director and headed out the main gate amid much front seat giggling. When out of sight a short time later, we made a sharp left turn in our battered four-wheel drive and headed overland off-track into the foothills. A high barbed-wire fence on an elevated ridge announced that we were now at the site of the original track bed.

A few kilometres further on the fence produced a rusty gate which miraculously opened with some small manipulation (no lock, just a rusty bolt to go with the rusty gate). Off we set along the bed, arriving a short distance later at a dilapidated, faded sign indicating the exact meeting point. Along the way back we stopped occasionally and picked up some of the old iron spikes from 1869 that had been flung aside by the Corps of Engineers in their hurry to lift up the track rails. Apparently, the spikes represented no added-value to their endeavour. Their loss was our gain and I was later presented with one of these historically significant spikes mounted in a specially-made (by one of my Irish hosts) glass case, together with an inscription to mark the date of our little joint (ad)venture. That was the kind of spirit of independence the Irish community in Utah loved to show on occasion!

I realise now I could write a separate volume on my West Coast experiences; it would have twelve chapters to cover each of the western states that I managed to visit, Alaska being the exception. I almost got there, too, except Mary McAleese decided she should visit Seattle just two months before I was due to leave for my next posting. Such is life and I did enjoy accompanying her on her visits which included Microsoft (which has a significant Irish community of workers) and Boeing, and the largest single span factory building in the world.

And that visit was important for two other reasons. Firstly, John Keane lived up to the belief that he would make a great Honorary Consul for Washington State, to which role he has since served with distinction, as they say. Secondly, I managed to convince both the President and my Ambassador in DC at the time, Noel Fahey, that 'Butte, America', an average-sized mining town in the middle of the Great Sky State of Montana, was unique in its connections to Ireland. President McAleese decided that her next trip would be to Montana which took place in 2006. I was delighted to hear back from my many friends there that she had said it had been her best visit to the States ever!

Indeed, now that I think of it, I could probably write an entire book about the Irish in Montana. I had heard before being appointed Consulate General that Butte was a special place for the Irish after listening to Kerry-born Dr. Paddy Moriarty, long-time successful CEO of the ESB and related to the equally famous GAA commentator, Mícheál Ó Muircheartaigh. Paddy was on a visit to DC in 1988 with Minister Ray Burke. Unfortunately, relations between Minister and public servant were quite fraught by the time they got to DC. In one of our rare tranquil moments after the minister had withdrawn to his room, Paddy regaled me with the links between the Allihies and other small hard-rock mining communities of southwest Ireland and Butte, Montana.

In the mid-nineteenth century, as the largest copper-mining operation in the northern hemisphere and a magnet for immigrants escaping the calamity of the famine, Butte became so well-known that those looking to go there referred to it as 'Butte, America'. For those who want to know more, Dr David Emmons, eminent historian of the University of Montana at Missoula, has written the definitive history of the Butte Irish and their huge contribution not only to the local community but to the Irish in America. I met Dave on several of the trips I made to Montana, and I am pleased to say that I still count many of the residents of Butte among my good friends, in particular, Mitsy Daily and her large extended family. I may well write a book about her as well, as she is some woman.

One or two meetings spring to mind. There was Father Sarsfield O'Sullivan, son of a County Cork miner, who became local parish priest; he recalled the time his father sheltered Éamon de Valera in 1919 when he was on the run from the British authorities after escaping, with Michael Collins' help, from Stafford Gaol. It seems Dev knew well the Irish connection to Butte even if the authorities did not, and stayed for several months with Father Sarsfield's family. I was delighted to hear that President McAleese visited Father Sars, as he was known locally, when she visited Butte.

And John O'Shea, a descendant of a Cork miner who was a miner himself. John regaled me with stories, many of them, alas, about disasters from the pits as he showed me around the Butte mines and the Anaconda smelter a couple of miles distant. He referred to large rocks as D's, indicating that many ones of similar size had fallen from mine shaft roofs, killing unfortunate miners who happened to get in their way. And I remember at one pithead entrance he picked up a large, shiny stone and said, 'This one is called "Leverrite!"' with a smile on his face. I picked it up and asked was it valuable, thinking it might have been overlooked when the mine was closed. John replied it's called 'Lever-rite' as in 'Leave it right there!' and we both laughed.

When John was made redundant, he and a group of fellow miners began construction of what is now the famous 'Our Lady of the Rockies', a massive white metal statue placed on the edge of the butte outcrop that lent the town its name (see photo section 1). The statue was so tall and the butte so steep that it required the loan of an Army Corps of Engineers heavy-lift helicopter to take the five sections of statue up. Even then, I am told, it was touch and go as to whether the helicopter would manage to get the final piece aloft and in place.

Almost 1,000 people attended the State reception for the Irish Community in Seattle in May 2006, which took place in the ball-room of the large hotel where our delegation was staying. I had invited Irish communities from across the Western United States in the rare opportunity to meet an Irish President. But realisti-cally, I did not expect many to travel any long distances to do so. They did come from Spokane, which is on the eastern side of Washington State, and they also came up from Oregon. But I did not anticipate that a delegation of some 50 or so would travel all the way from Butte, on the far side of the Rockies!

And to save on accommodation costs, they drove through the night. I was delighted to see them in Seattle, and I made sure all were invited to a small reception area just beside the ballroom where the President was meeting VIPs before entering the main reception for her speech of welcome. I explained to my Butte friends the protocol formalities we would follow, that everyone should form an orderly queue, be presented by me to the President, shake her hand and move on quickly to allow the proceedings to finish on time.

What I did not anticipate was that the Butte contingent would go around twice, and each time pose for a photograph with the President! Mary McAleese took their behaviour with good humour and on entering the ballroom a short while later, began her speech by saying, 'I believe the entire town of Butte, America are here tonight!' Her words brought the house down with a mighty roar of approval!

The close connection of Butte to Ireland has to be experienced to appreciate it. O'Sullivan is the most popular name in the Butte phonebook; to distinguish him from other John Harringtons, John 'the Yank' Harrington was so-called because he was born in Butte, went to live in Kerry for several years and returned eventually to Butte.

Alas, Butte is also the site of the largest toxic waste clean-up by the EPA in the States. Set against the backdrop of rusting mine shaft heads and the great Butte of Our Lady, an open-cast pit, two miles wide and a mile deep is filled with bright orange sludge which has seeped into it over the years from the surrounding workings. This spectacular but lethal wound in the earth has now become a tourist destination as the town continues to shrink in its post-mining blight.

I also enjoyed the use of a former local hearse, a 1970s Cadillac limousine, put at my disposal to transport us around Butte and environs; it was a comfortable ride but I was happy to sit in the front seat rather than stretched out in the back!

Talking of Cadillacs, Beverley Hills is full of them, especially during the Oscar season. Minister John O'Donoghue and party were annual distinguished guests of the Irish Film Board and great company. He was also an excellent Minister to represent Ireland on these occasions. It was a pleasure to work with him

and to get into the studio boardrooms to meet the cinema mo-
guls who took decisions on locations for making movies, but the
best part was the inevitable tour of the famous movie lots, MGM,
Paramount, Universal etc. And I made a particularly good friend
in Donald Lee, an Executive Producer in Paramount, now living
in New York and a great friend of Ireland.

I recall the year, a good one for Ireland, when *Chernobyl Heart*,
featuring Adi Roche (more anon), took the Oscar for best short
documentary. Siobhán and myself were waiting outside the hotel lobby watching all the celebrities departing in their limos.
We didn't have tickets for the Kodak theatre ceremony itself, of
course – they were rarer than the proverbial hen's teeth – but we
weren't too sad as we were reliably informed that once seated
you were forbidden to move, or severely discouraged from doing so, even for calls of nature, for the four hour marathon that
the Oscars have become.

Out of the corner of my eye, I noticed a rather sorry looking
individual on crutches coming towards us; I was about to reach
into my pocket to hand him some loose change when I got a dig
in the ribs. 'That's Colin Farrell!' a breathless Siobhán exclaimed.
So I hastily returned said coins to where they were really needed,
in my pocket, and stuck out my hand. 'Hello,' I ventured. 'I am
the Irish Consul General, Dónal Denham, and this is my wife,
Siobhán.'

'Ah, hi Dónal! Pleased to meet you!

I asked hesitantly about the crutches. He stuck out his leg in
disgust, revealing a plaster below the chic-shabby jeans. 'Fell
off me horse, didn't I, and broke me leg! A nuisance I can tell
you!'

I asked if we could have a photo with him and he replied, 'Of course you can! Anything for my friend, the Consul!' (Colin was filming *Alexander* at the time.) And with that, photo posed and taken, he hopped with a hearty swing of his crutches into the back of his own limo to sweep him away to further fame down the road! Good guy, our Colin!

The Irish in Arizona were another fascinating group to visit, or groups I should say, as the notorious Irish lollipop fracture syndrome applied there (you know, when as a kid we would snap our balsa wood sticks in two, revealing a myriad of splintered ends). The first thing any Irish community committee does, as Brendan Behan famously noted, is to decide to split with as much venom as can last a lifetime and beyond. This was certainly the case in my early experience in Maryland and Virginia, but also as Consulate General in California, Washington and Oregon, and nowhere more enduringly so than Arizona.

One faction, the majority, who supported the Irish Centre of Phoenix, was under the iron grip of an octogenarian, William Howard 'Bill' O'Brien, who had served in World War II as a US marine and who had amassed a fortune from cattle ranching over the years. Bill owned an entire mountain north of Phoenix, called Camelback Mountain, picked up for a song after the war. He was cute enough to build himself a nice ranch on one side of it and sell off some of the land on the lower slopes for an exclusive spa and private housing development and to retire on the proceeds.

He was a hoot. Apparently, he had served on the first US naval vessel to arrive at the port of Nagasaki within days of the atom bomb being dropped on the city. Bill recalls that he and a friend sneaked off the ship into the city without anyone noticing. They had a good look around at the devastation but realised that,

in the circumstances, there wasn't much reason to hang around
and so returned to their ship. Arriving back at the quayside,
they saw before them seemingly endless barriers of yellow tape
everywhere with warnings about something called 'radiation'.
They were then surrounded by Military Police and marched off
to a room in the bowels of the ship where they spent the rest of
their cruise in complete isolation. On return to the US mainland
they were flown to the nearest naval hospital for further exam-
ination but as neither Bill nor his friend showed any symptoms
of radiation sickness, they were eventually discharged and subsequently returned to civilian life. However, twice a year for the
rest of his long life (Bill was 80 when he recounted this tale), he
and his friend, who also lived a full and normal life, were flown
by the navy to Bethesda Naval Hospital to be checked for any
signs of radiation damage caused by that early visit to Nagasaki!
(Bill, RIP, passed away a few years ago at the great age of 92).

Unfortunately, Bill was used to getting his own way on just
about everything, including on how the Irish Centre, of which
he was inordinately proud as the major donor to its new cus-
tom-built location, should be run. Other people, including a gent
by the name of Art O'Hagan, had a profound disagreement with
Bill about fundraising and the rest is history. The dispute became
bitter and personal and eventually political, with Art pushing a
strong Sinn Féin line which left him in the cold with most of the
Phoenix Irish community of the time. But Art had good business
connections so it meant that the Consul General, when visiting
from San Francisco, had to tread carefully, not letting the one
know about contacts with the other. I eventually stopped going
there as it became too awkward and my frequent attempts to
heal the rift were to no avail.

Likewise, in San Diego, it proved challenging to keep the peace between the warring factions within the Irish community. There was a wealthy clique who, in general, took no great interest in visits from the Consulate. One person, however, who was outstandingly supportive with his time and commitment was, as I mentioned, Rob Mullaly, a TCD alumni and, subsequently, a good friend. Rob and myself worked hard to establish a positive Irish profile and to help the Irish 'J1-oners' who invaded southern California every summer. There was a lack of tolerance for the drinking culture they brought with them; no one under 21 was legally allowed to imbibe alcohol but many tried anyway. It invariably led to clashes with local law enforcement. We tried our best to minimise the friction, but it wasn't easy or entirely successful.

Other characters I came across in my travels included Daithi O'Longaigh and Barry Glass in Portland. Daithi was a pleasant person in the City of Portland's Bridges Department, of which there were a great many. Barry had his own life assurance agency which, by all indications, provided him with quite a tidy annual income. He wasn't married at the time but had many girlfriends vying for his attentions, though Barry studiously avoided any threat to his single status. He was Jewish, though not fanatically so, Dublin-born and always referring fondly to 'da Mammy'. I subsequently discovered, after he let it slip, that there was a previously unhappy marriage and a teenage son in his background; Barry was coy when it came to his personal history. Whenever I asked him how business was, he invariably would reply, 'Oh, business is bad!' which he once explained was his superstitious way of saying all was going well without tempting fate.

Daithi had a very pleasant, tolerant spouse and a family of four young children yet his one goal in life, having revived a long-dormant local chapter of the Ancient Order of Hibernians, was to have a Celtic cross erected in Portland to the memory of the Irish post-famine 'pioneers' who crossed the great plains, those dry-land oceans with their amber waves of grain, who by-passed easier opportunities to settle into a new life in such places as Montana (see the Butte America story above) in favour of a hazardous crossing of the Rockies to Washington state and to Oregon, there to stop basically from exhaustion for the rest of their lives.

Daithi's proposition of a Celtic cross memorial to those who were victims of The Famine as well as to those brave souls who escaped from it was a nice, if rather orthodox, idea. But it wasn't enough for Daithi to create a memorial using local materials and skills. No, Daithi had to commission a traditional Irish sculptor to replicate a Celtic cross made of Irish granite and to have it transported, lock, stock and extremely heavy barrel, to Portland. To begin the process, Daithi had obtained the grant of a small site in a nice parkland location, Mount Cavalry RC Cemetery, where many of the Irish of Oregon lay buried, just on the out-skirts of the city.

That was where the matter rested when I was first approached by Daithi on a visit to Oregon, shortly after my arrival as Con-sul General. I was intrigued as to how Daithi would achieve his goal and managed to obtain a modest cultural grant to help him begin the process of commissioning. An order was put in with Brendan McGloin in Donegal for one finely chiselled Celtic cross in Irish granite and work began. It took over ten years of snail-like progress but Daithi's determination finally paid off with delivery overland of a fine but horrendously expensive cross. In the meantime, Daithi had sweated blood to convince every wealthy Oregonian he came across, and the state didn't boast a huge reservoir of successful business types willing to donate in return for a tax break. I had left before the memorial was officially unveiled by President McAleese in 2008, suitably appropriate in the middle of an Oregon blizzard! Despite the inclement weather, over 400 attended the ceremony. It was the first visit by a serving Irish president to Oregon though, as I had discovered previously, de Valera was hounded out of the city by local Ku Klux Klan elements in 1919 while on his US fundraising tour (I also came across him in Brown's Hotel in Denver, Colorado; the hotel boasts a menu card especially printed in honour of his visit there and signed by him).

On another occasion, I was invited by the local University of Oregon to say a few words of welcome to Bono who was guest speaker at an annual event on campus. I was a bit in awe but managed to get out a *cúpla focail* and even have a photo of the great one to prove it! Both Daithi and Barry were my witnesses.

I met and fell (figuratively-speaking) in love with Maureen Hurley, mother of 12 children and a self-employed travel agent in Spokane, whose favourite pastime was to take a group on tour to Ireland every year. Maureen wasn't high fallutin or famous like Spokane's most famous son, Harry Lillis 'Bing' Crosby.

Maureen took me to see the first-floor window that Bing Crosby, law student at Gonzaga University, was alleged to have pushed a grand piano through in a fit of rage; this, needless to say, is local lore but it is true that Bing 'dropped out' of Gonzaga, much to his mother's chagrin, just a year shy of graduation. His budding music career was already blossoming with a group called

'The Musicaladers' in the early 1920s which distracted him from his studies, according to legend. He made up for it in retrospect by becoming a generous donor to the university; it sports a Bing Crosby Library with the most extensive collection of his papers and disc recordings. Mind you, a glance at their website recently did not mention him as a distinguished alumnus; obviously, even the J's are snobbish on occasion, with only graduates receiving that distinction.

One of the stranger places I visited as Consul General was New Mexico. I received an invitation one day from an English Literature professor at the University of New Mexico in Albuquerque who happened to be one of the many Joycean experts with tenuous direct connections to Ireland which the States seems to produce. In this case, he was a genuine, published Joyce scholar, invited to international events to declaim on the great one and his works. We had, at the time, a DFA touring exhibition on Joyce involving self-standing panels and our friend in Albuquerque had requested hosting it on campus, which we were happy to do.

Prior to my visit, as was my wont, I researched the existence of local Irish organisations and was surprised to discover one such in Albuquerque which boasted a membership of some 300. I immediately made contact. My liaison was Chuck McLaughlin, initially suspicious and slightly hostile – he was yet another Sinn Féin supporter – but who later became a good friend. The '300' turned out to be quite a few less than advertised, and almost none I met that first time were first or even second generation Irish, but they were welcoming as always.

I also travelled up to Santa Fe, the gorgeous state capital with a substantial artistic heritage and active community (to my eternal regret, however, I did not go beyond, to Taos, the artists' epicentre, where there is a little-known collection of nude paintings by D.H. Lawrence, he of Lady Chatterley fame). In Santa Fe, I failed to meet the Democrat Governor who was too busy electioneering and cancelled my courtesy call at short notice, but I did meet an extraordinary character, James O'Hara, who, I discovered, wrote some of the best poetry I have read. It was, as they say, strong meat, not to everybody's taste, but I still hope he gets the recognition he deserves and publication bragging rights to go with it.

Wyoming is almost the last outpost of the real Wild West; cowboys, horses and lots of cattle on the move. It was interesting to visit but there isn't a lot to see beyond the enormous ranches and tiny towns linking them. Not too many native Indians or Irish around. Likewise, Idaho was scenically beautiful, and Boise has a small Irish community which was clustered around a large HP facility (the computer company, not the sauce!) and the university. We had a good session of the AGM of the American Conference of Irish Studies West there, I recall.

There are so many other places and people I would like to mention. Father Brendan McBride and Celine Kennelly of the San Francisco Pastoral Centre were amazing in their dedication, effort and patience in supporting the San Francisco Irish community, especially but certainly not exclusively the recently arrived. Many of the lonely, older Irish residents benefited from their care and attention. That is in itself a story for another time, but I am glad to say that I was the first Consul General to make successfully their case for financial support for the Centre from Irish government resources.

In many ways, what we pioneered together in San Francisco became the template for assisting the Irish communities across the US, though those on the East Coast may huff and puff about their relative size and importance. Indeed, one of the first things to strike me, on arriving in San Francisco, was how different the Western US is from the East Coast, and how the two are in turn so different from the vast area that is 'middle America'. And that difference translates into a deep-seated rivalry between the Irish communities of the West and the East; they have literally different and diverging oral traditions and histories, quite at variance with the monolithic interpretation of 'Irish America' by most Irish at home.

One of our high-profile visitors to the Western US consular territory was Brian Cowen who came for the St. Patrick's Day celebrations in 2004. He was easy to deal with, wanting to spend as much of his free time as allowed meeting old friends from Clara who were long-time residents of the City. As he was staying in a fancy downtown hotel, this involved his slipping away out the back door of the hotel with his local guides after the official programme ended, usually about 10.00 pm and not being seen again until breakfast time, quite often just before the breakfast service ended. I recall that he would sit in the splendid elegance of the old hotel and order a hearty US equivalent of the Full Irish. And yes, he was often 'hoarse'. I was witness to his daily briefing from our esteemed Secretary General of the time, Dermot Gallagher. Dermot had me open up the Consulate at 6.00 am each morning of the visit, together with a willing local staff member. Dermot would go through all the correspondence that had come through overnight from HQ (eight hours' time difference), draft replies for us to send and work on the Minister's remarks.

Dermot and I would then take copies of the Irish press summaries especially tailored for the Minister in true Foreign Affairs fashion (no effort was too much to keep a Minister swaddled and happy) back to the hotel where we would wait for the ministerial levee over breakfast (one morning, he actually came into the hotel lobby, dropped there by his Clara minders after a full night on the tiles). It was hilarious. Brian would order his full breakfast; Dermot would approach and ask for a few minutes' audience. The Minister would oblige. Dermot would then, in true Sir Humphrey style, raise those issues he wanted Brian's blessing on in an obsequiously soft manner for which he was renowned. The Minister would invariably spot the real, hidden agenda which Dermot had carefully tried to disguise in the middle of more innocuous matters. Like a patient fly fisherman, Cowen would reel in Dermot, playing him for all he was worth and enjoying every moment of Dermot's wriggling before inexorably confessing to the Minister his true motives for recommending such-and-such a strategy.

On one such occasion, Brian began to laugh, and Dermot started to smile broadly. Brian turned to me, a mere acolyte a table away, and said to me in a loud voice, 'Donal, let that be a lesson to you; never try to bullshit a bullshitter!'

I am grateful to Dermot, Brian Cowen, Mary Harney and others for all the kindness they showed me and for allowing my name to go forward as the first resident Ambassador of Ireland to Lithuania in September 2005. It was hard to leave behind the City by the Bay and so many good friendships both there and across the entire consular area I covered, but being appointed Ambassador for the first time in my career was an offer I couldn't refuse (Mary Harney wondered if I would not prefer another year in San Francisco, but that would have meant risking what I felt was an irresistible opportunity).

Before leaving San Francisco, I hosted a reception, the first of its kind, to mark our 2004 EU Presidency. Normally, there is very little contact or cooperation among EU partners in consular posts; in fact, the prevailing atmosphere is usually competitive. But I was determined to get some profile for the EU locally, despite an apparent lack of interest from the Commission office in DC. That bunch seemed to think the US started and ended within the confines of the Beltway freeway, which marked the outer psychological boundary of Washington DC and suburbs.

So, as I did back in 1980 in Lusaka, I invited my EU colleagues resident in San Francisco to come together for the first time to talk about matters in common and to participate in the reception I planned to mark our Presidency. All the Member States had consulates, mostly career but a few honorary, on the west coast, either in San Francisco or in Los Angeles, and the split was about 70 per cent in San Francisco's favour which was helpful.

The EU reception was a spectacular success, with each Consul standing beside their national flag and each speaking for a few minutes before the assembled distinguished guests, mainly local dignitaries and business contacts. I was glad I had made the effort and it led to successor EU Presidencies taking their role more seriously and holding at least two meetings during each one. These occasions also came to the notice of the EU Commission in DC who belatedly began to show an interest in using this putative network for publicity and west coast visits.

The one thing I will say now about the EU bureaucracy is that the rest of the world is safe in the complete and utter absence of initiative, creativity or imagination on the part of Brussels, relying almost entirely on the constituent Member States in the field to generate any sort of new thinking and proactive approach. God help Brussels without the UK!

Life has its ups and downs, as we all know from our own direct experience. For me, personally, and for our family, one of the saddest was the death of my nephew, Killian Own, aged 9, in 2003, after a four-year battle with cancer. Killian was the twin child of my sister, Grainne, and her husband Clay. Killian's twin is Garrett and he has an elder brother, Pierce, and a younger brother, Finnian, also known as Finn. I use the present tense for we all feel Killian is very much still with us in his amazing spirit, or soul presence, as are all those deceased relatives and friends who live on in our thoughts and memories.

Despite the brutal sorrow which his parents still feel, they picked themselves up. My sister Grainne's response, with Clay's help and massive support from Killian's siblings, was to found a unique charity, Curing Kids' Cancer, to raise funds for research into childhood leukaemia and a cure for same. In the 15 short years of its existence, the charity has raised over $20 million to this end. Bravo Grainne, Clay, Pierce, Garrett and Finn!

I can't complete this chapter without mentioning the exploits of Fred Forster, a 65-year-old Irishman who had made a serious amount of money from buying up companies in distress, rehabilitating them, and then selling them on at a tidy profit. I met Fred by accident on a flight to Ireland; otherwise, I don't think I would have come across him as he had developed an incredibly low profile in San Francisco.

Fred's one indulgence was rugby. At 65, he was still a playing member and President of Newbridge Rugby Club and the time I met him he was on his way to a game in Kildare. Fred told me he had married his long-suffering spouse, Victoria, during half time at a particular match. He didn't reveal what the final score was!

But Fred's skill at rugby, as well as jam-making, another hobby he had developed late in life, did not extend to driving a car. The first time he picked me up to take me to his home, a modest enough ranch house in the valley south of the city, we had to drive through the city in rush-hour traffic, itself a hazardous experience at the best of times. Fred's idea of dealing with multiple lanes of busy traffic – buses, trucks, cars were all the same to him – was to zig-zag continuously, right and left, in and out of lanes, hand stuck out to indicate occasionally but usually his manoeuvres were not signalled in advance. He ignored the resulting cacophony of honking horns with a smile and a jaunty wave as he focused on the next negotiation of obstacles ahead. I was never more terrified in my life!

There was never a dull moment in that amazing posting, and I have many more episodes of life there yet to tell, but they will have to await another time. Our four plus years were over before we knew it!

So we packed up our bags yet again, for the eighth time, and headed back east to, for me, an exciting new possibility, establishing, for the second time in my career an outpost for Ireland. Vilnius was my destination and my destiny for the next five years and beyond…

Postscript: Since writing the above, I have learnt of the death of Fred Forster at the venerable age of 85; no doubt he is now on St. Peter's XV and making everyone up there his best Fred's Jam!

Chapter 8

Lithuania and Belarus

Lithuania, another Irish Mission opening; 'on the wall' at the edge of the former Evil Empire; the complex history of Lithuania; Jewish Vilnius, the Holocaust and the Ghetto; Ireland, Lithuania and a moving Marian statue; inside an intercontinental ballistic missile (ICBM) silo; diplomatic lists and an inspector calls; Aunty Mary Mac visits, ice-creams all round; comparing Landsbergis, Adamkus and Grybauskaite; Belarus, taking Minsk back from Moscow; the ghost of Lee Harvey Oswald; massive Irish contribution to Chernobyl's future generations; EHU, university in exile; meeting Lukashenka, the last dictator, face to face; my last EU Presidency.

So it was off on another adventure on behalf of the Department of Foreign Affairs (and Trade, as it later became). Though it was hard to leave the Western US behind us, the prospect of my first official posting as an Ambassador of Ireland, the pinnacle of my ambition, was almost beyond words. And to open a new Embassy made it all the more exciting.

Permission had been given by the Department of Finance to the Department of Foreign Affairs and Trade to open resident missions in all the new EU Member States, following its enlargement from 15 to 25 by virtue of ten new Central and Eastern European adherents under our 2004 Presidency. That permission was made conditional in the immediate post-presidency after-math of budget expenditure reductions which was *de riguer* prac-tice in Merrion Street. It meant that we could open, in theory, as many new missions as we wished on condition that they were established and run 'within existing resources'.

This caused a temporary delay as the Department allowed the dust to settle before proceeding as before with the opening of a resident mission in the capitals of the new Member States where we did not already have one on the ground; for some strange reason, we had opened one in Tallinn, Estonia well before en-largement. To comply with the Finance restriction, I was told to keep a low profile and to engage local staff using an employment agency so that we would not incur any long-term contractual ob-ligations by adding to Departmental staff numbers and resultant salary-related and pension costs. So, a Third Secretary and my-self arrived without publicity in Vilnius in September 2005. We pitched tent in a 'business hub' with shared services and began the slow process of recruiting local staff and finding a location both for the office and the official residence.

I was determined to do it properly for the long haul and I had the unconditional backing from my spouse in doing so. We had learnt lessons from our time in Zambia, also a 'new build' operation, in 1980. We knew it required patience and planning, and the cooperation of the Department's principal architect, Mark McSwiney, with whom I had worked on many previous occasions in Paris, Zambia and in Washington DC on a major embassy building overhaul.

We lodged in a small apartment belonging to a local hotel and I set out to find an office location. This was easy compared to finding suitable residential accommodation; Vilnius had been ravaged by 50 years of Soviet occupation and housing stock was extremely low in absolute terms. Most locals lived in the all-pervasive Stalinist-era workers' apartment blocks which ringed the city suburbs like a chain of forts, probably with that very intention in mind by his architects.

A Brief History of Lithuania

Vilnius was an old city with wonderful baroque-style buildings, especially the many churches it constructed when it was the seventeenth century royal family capital of the Polish Empire (I counted 32 spires on its mediaeval skyline at one point). Poland and Ukraine provided the bodies and Lithuania the ruling family. That empire stretched from the Baltic to the Black Sea and Vilnius was quite a wealthy trading cross-roads between East (Russia) and West (the Hanseatic League coastal cities, Memel being the nearest, and the Swedish Empire), North (Riga and beyond) and South (the Ottoman Empire). The Polish Empire was subsumed by its burgeoning Russian neighbour, with St. Petersburg appearing in the early 1700s.

Lithuania was then ravaged by Napoleon on his way back from Moscow – he lost some 90,000 battle-weary troops to typhoid and cholera epidemics while in Vilnius and many are buried in unmarked graves. He left for Paris with the remnants of his once great army (some 10,000 remained), chased by the Russian Army (one of the Marshals was an Irish mercenary exile named O'Rourke who was given a large tract of land near Grodno, now in Western Belarus, but more of that connection later). Vilnius became a rather sleepy provincial Polish-speaking city for much of the next 100 years.

World War I fought, as the allies proclaimed, on behalf of Europe's small nations, brought more depredation. The Treaty of Versailles, that most unsatisfactory of settlements, saw Lithuania and its two Baltic neighbours established as independent republics, but not before a Polish nationalist occupation led by the famous Polish Marshal, Jozef Pilsudski. Versailles re-established an independent Poland also, whose first Prime Minister was Jan Paderewski who was also, of course, a noted musician and composer, and who was one of the more able of the Versailles participants.

Thus, in 1919 Lithuania became a small but quite prosperous inter-war republic with its capital at Kaunas, also an old medi-aeval city in the centre of the country, linked by the Neman and Neris rivers to the small (99 kilometres) but perfectly formed Baltic coast to the northeast at Klaipeda, formerly Memel. Kaunas was visited by Napoleon on his way to Moscow in 1810–11 and still has some scars to prove it. Kaunas is now a rather lively place in contrast with its neglect under Soviet occupation. One interesting connection with Ireland was an attempt by certain businessmen in Lithuania to establish a peat bog and turf in-dustry and who sought to develop links with Irish counterparts. Meanwhile, Vilnius remained part of Poland and both had sig-nificant Jewish populations.

All this was to change utterly with the advent of World War II, known to the Russians as the Great Patriotic War. Lithuania was briefly occupied by Russia on the outbreak of war, part of the secret Molotov-Ribbentrop Pact which saw much of the rel-atively new Central and Eastern European republics divided between Germany and Russia. It was then invaded early on by the northern flank thrust of Hitler's armies of the east, and the

Russians were driven back beyond Minsk, 120 kilometres direct-ly east of Vilnius.

In a short interval in 1940, between the Russians leaving and the Germans arriving, certain of the nationalist zealots in the Kaunas community took it upon themselves to carry out one of the most horrific of the many pogroms the local Jewish commu-nity was to suffer. Hatchets and blunt implements were used to massacre a large group of local Jewish business people and their family members in the city centre. This was to be the first of many such vicious and unprovoked attacks on Jewish neighbours across the country. With Nazi occupation, ghettos were quick-ly established in Kaunas, Vilnius and other provincial centres; by the end of the German occupation almost 100,000 Lithuanian Jews had been exterminated during the Holocaust. Lithuania has the unenviable legacy of being the country with the highest per-centage (96 per cent) of its pre-war Jewish community to perish in the Holocaust.

My interest in twentieth century history meant I was fortunate to make the acquaintance early on in Vilnius of Dr. Dovid Katz, a Brooklyn-born and raised Jewish rabbi and Yiddish scholar, whose family had lived for many generations in Lithuania before being driven out by a late-nineteenth century Russian pogrom in what was then all part of Poland. Dovid later introduced me to Efraim Zuroff, the well-known Director of the Simon Wiesenthal Center in Jerusalem.

Many of the Irish Jewish community share that origin, in-cluding the famous Copeland family of tailors. Dovid became a close friend and mentor for all things Jewish. He established the Centre for Yiddish Studies at Oxford University; after some academic intrigue, he left Oxford and came to Vilnius and did the same. His intention in setting up a Centre for Yiddish Studies at the University of Vilnius, itself 15 years older than my alma mater, Trinity College Dublin, was to rekindle a local knowledge and love for the Yiddish language in what had been a major hub for it prior to 1945. I should add that when the Russians re-took Vilnius in 1944, over 50 per cent of the population of the city and surrounds was ethnic Polish, of whom 20 per cent plus had been Jewish prior to the extermination of its ghetto in 1943. By 1945, Vilnius was largely ethnic Lithuanian, with a tiny minority of remaining Jews and a small minority of Poles. In fact, Vilnius has Polish-speaking schools and a number of villages in the immediate vicinity of the city where Polish is spoken. At the elections in 2010, it elected a small Polish Party representative to both the national and to the European parliaments.

Dovid is a brilliant academic, the best in his field, but like many academics can be tenacious on occasion, as I soon discovered. He is now living off his writing – he has published copious volumes of learned tomes on Yiddish and Jewish history – and international lecturing, while renting an elegant nineteenth century Vilnius apartment crammed with books (and owning a small house in North Wales whose walls are similarly book-lined).

I spent many an evening attending soirees which he hosts from time to time, always filled with eccentric types and eclectic and interesting conversations, many started, few finished. And it was Dovid who introduced me to Fania Brankovsky (see photo section 2), an amazing woman.

Fania was born in the early 1920s into a Jewish family of five siblings, living in the countryside south of Vilnius for several generations. Fania was one of many Jewish teenagers and their families who were rounded up in 1941 and herded into

Vilnius city centre, itself the site of one of the largest mediaeval synagogues in the northern hemisphere, and already home to many Jewish artisans, tailors, watchmakers and glass-blowers. The occupying Nazis found it easy enough to build large wooden barriers at the end of the maze of narrow streets which made up the Old Town of Vilnius to create two ghettos (one an overspill) after rounding up the local Jewish population. Those streets are still there, largely intact despite centuries of marauding foreign forces and the best efforts under Soviet rule in the 1960s to bulldoze them to make way for a motorway running through the city centre, just as they did in Kaliningrad, formerly Konigsberg, a fine Hanseatic city on the Baltic, the birth place of Emmanuel Kant. Dovid gives a unique tour of the Ghetto for those who have an interest in the Holocaust.

In September 1943, the Ghetto was liquidated under the command of Oberscharführer Bruno Kittel, German Governor of Vilnius. A similar process of the obliteration of the Jewish inhabitants was carried out in Kaunas and at other locations in Lithuania, often with enthusiastic support and involvement from members of the local community eager to eliminate their middle class Jewish neighbours and to take possession of their land and other resources. While such an obscene, dehumanising abomination was widespread throughout Europe, especially though not exclusively in the east where the Holocaust was executed in a totally cruel, vindictive way, Lithuania is held up as a particularly egregious example of Nazi war crimes against humanity, mainly against the Jewish community.

Fania's parents and four siblings were all shipped by a goods wagon train a few short kilometres outside the city boundary to the Paneriai Forest where they were forced to excavate large pits from a former oil-storage terminal and to witness mass executions before they, too, were lined up and mown down by German execution squads. Over 40,000 suffered such a fate. Fania was one of just a few hundred Ghetto survivors who escaped the confines of the Old Town through an ancient sewage tunnel system and who fled into the forest to the south of the city to find refuge among communist guerrilla bands.

Fania took me to her remote hiding place deep in one of the many wooded groves surrounding Vilnius, long since neglected and overgrown after what was then 50 years of Soviet occupation and a subsequent 15 years of nationalist independence. In neither case did the regime wish to acknowledge, much less preserve, the historic contribution of local communist partisans to liberation from the Nazis. I was privileged to be her witness to these awful conditions under which she survived the Great Patriotic War. Fania went on to fight against the Nazis herself, and following the end of the war lived a modest life under Russian Soviet rule in one of the many Stalinist residential blocks (shades of Ballymun Towers) as mentioned earlier. Fania became Librarian and Archivist at the Centre for Yiddish Studies at the University of Vilnius upon its founding. I was also proud to be invited to host a reception at our residence in her honour in 2008. She is an example of human dignity at its best, of the will to resist evil and to conquer it.

And Fania was not alone among the survivors of the Holocaust to have chosen to return to Vilnius; Dovid quietly invited me to join him on Wednesday afternoons for a regular series of calls he made to other Holocaust survivors still living in Vilnius. Their stories were vivid and heart-rending, and yet so fresh in their memories, despite living under 50 years of communism;

they hated the one and tolerated the other. Dovid was recording their experiences lest anyone forget the genocide that befell the Jewish community for simply being Jewish. Holocaust remembrance is unique and must not be confused with other horrific crimes against humanity.

But I digress. In my time in Lithuania, every day was interesting as one came to learn so much about the realities of 50 years of communist rule, much more complex and less evil than a distant view would lead one to believe. It was true that Churchill's famous 'Iron Curtain' was as much a veil of ignorance as it was a barrier to dialogue. And it took two sides to fight the infamous Cold War. More contact between European states of the West and of the East might have avoided much of the prejudice and bigotry on all counts.

I distinctly remember, on our first weekend in Vilnius, asking an estate agent who had been showing us some of the very few properties for rent available on the market what it was like under Russian domination? She replied without a moment's hesitation that 'everyone was a thief, we all stole from our rulers'.

That seemed fair enough to me, so I followed up by asking what she had been doing, since there had obviously been no need for estate agents.

'I was a librarian in those days...'

'So,' I interrupted, 'you stole books?'

'Oh no, nothing like that! I stole time! I came in late and went home early.' I felt suitably chastened.

The Prime Minister when I first arrived was Algirdas Brazauskas, the last Secretary of the Communist Party of Lithuania prior to re-independence in 1989 and the first person to be appointed as President in 1993, much to the chagrin of the

Music Professor, Vytautas Landsbergis, a scholarly but formal individual who is acknowledged to have led the protests (such as the human chain demonstration linking Vilnius to Tallinn via Riga) and the independence movement, the Sajūdis, of which more anon. Professor Landsbergis was the one who negotiated the break with Moscow under Boris Yeltsin; he led the nationalist Lithuanian Conservative Party and was the first Lithuanian Prime Minister.

However, Brazauskas beat him to become the first president, thus cementing a life-long enmity. When, for example, Brazauskas died in 2010, he was denied a Catholic funeral service in Vilnius Cathedral which would have been his due under State protocol. As my office balcony overlooked the Cathedral and the route to the cemetery, I can record from direct observation that the funeral cortege slowed down for a split second as the hearse passed the Cathedral, the closest Brazauskas ever came to entering its doors.

One of the many slights – for this hatred was indeed mutual – was the harassment of both Catholic clergy and laity by local communist authorities. For example, the clergy was infiltrated by Communist Party members in order to denounce those in the church who were active in opposing Soviet rule – and there were many. As in so many other ways in Lithuania, Polish influence dominated history and society. Thus, upon John Paul II becoming Pope Lithuania's Catholic Church was the focal point of nationalist fervour and opposition to communism.

Ireland, Lithuania and a Moving Marian Statue

Lithuania has its own Marian apparition site, the equivalent of Knock, Lourdes, Fatima, Medjugorje, Walsingham and others, at

Šiluva. Šiluva is the site of a Marian apparition in the fifteenth century and host to a famous icon that has been described as 'Lithuania's greatest treasure'. In the side chapel of the Basilica which houses the icon is a four-foot statue of Our Lady, smuggled from Dublin in 1983 in a tale that could rank with any cold war novel. At is origin is a Dublin lawyer of intense Catholic faith, T. F. O'Mahony, who, starting in 1977, offered the statue to the Lithuanian Catholic Church. The Soviet authorities turned down his request and many attempts over the subsequent years to send the statue to Šiluva were thwarted, despite diplomatic and other lobbying. Finally, in 1983, through the efforts of the Polish and Lithuanian Catholic Church communities in London, the now infamous statue was allowed to be taken under priestly escort to its resting place in Šiluva.

Novenas for the freedom of Lithuania and the demise of the Soviet Union began on the thirteenth of every month thereafter in front of that same statue. And, lo and behold, the rest is history! So we may claim that divine intervention, inspired by Our Lady of Šiluva, assisted in a modest way by an Irish statue of the Blessed Virgin that moved, in this case from Dublin via London to Moscow and back to Šiluva, was responsible for the release of Lithuania from 50 years of Soviet occupation!

Whoever struck the first blow, and the old Russian proverb says that it is the second blow that starts the war, the Catholic Church was the ultimate victor in the tussle for the minds and souls of Lithuanian society, which even today is deeply religious with a hierarchy that is steely conservative in its approach to matters moral and political.

In the meantime, many of Vilnius's beautiful baroque churches were either closed or altered by the communist authorities.

Thus, the Cathedral became a national art gallery and, ironically, when restored to original use still retained much of the valuable religious artwork that hung on its walls for 50 years of Soviet rule, while the wonderful and ancient Franciscan Friary church was turned into a tractor store, with much wilful and sacrilegious damage caused to the fine interior (ISIS were by no means the only cultural terrorists and post-Patriotic War communism didn't lick it off the grass, as they say). The city centre Jesuit church was also closed, and its interior destroyed beyond recovery. Typically, the Jesuits just went for a complete, rather garish makeover, whereas the Franciscans, true to their roots, are doggedly refusing to give up the fight to achieve a full and authentic restoration, even as the extent of the project threatens to overwhelm them.

This led me to uncover the resilience, resistance and patience of Lithuanian society when it comes to recovering the legacy of centuries of fine architectural achievements in the Old Town of Vilnius, the largest in Europe, and a place I never tired of show-ing off to visitors during my five years as a resident. There were essentially three phases of restoration activity on an immense scale and with little in the way of resources.

Firstly, were the buildings as inherited after the 50 years of Soviet rule, often dilapidated and mostly in roofless ruins, with rain and weather damage both inside and out. Restoration re-quired many months, even years of repairs.

There was then a second, extended phase, with many semi-finished examples peppering the urban landscape. I initially wondered why there was a certain amount of activity followed by a hiatus that could last for many months. Then I realised that such work was primarily funded by small annual allocations of limited financial and human resources which were suspended when funds ran out for that particular year and would not resume unless the next small funding tranche materialised, no matter what stage the restoration had reached.

The third phase was a revelatory celebration of the final product, a big, often community-organised party to record the full and final restoration. Thus, Vilnius was a city of ruins, of rebuildings and pristine reclamation, always fascinating to observe in its continuous evolution. And, indeed, much of the restoration has now been completed to the credit of all concerned. I love Vilnius and would recommend it as a seriously attractive destination.

I was fortunate to locate a fine space for our Embassy Chancery after several months of concentrated search. In fact, the address, as I subsequently discovered when presenting visiting cards to locals, could not have been more prestigious: 1 Gedimino Prospekt. 'One Gedimino', as it was colloquially known, is the headquarters of the Sąjūdis, Lithuania's equivalent of pre-1922 Sinn Féin cum IRB. Thus, the human chain event I mentioned earlier began at One Gedimino and Landsbergis had his office there, one floor above our Embassy. His office is still carefully preserved, much as he left it in 1989, by the faithful remnants of the Sąjūdis movement, rapidly aging, unbending in their time-frozen outlook, guardians of the purity of Lithuanian civilisation, culture and language, as if Soviet domination had never occurred. They were our neighbours and became our friends.

Our own landlords were, in fact, Irish, eminently respectable and paid their taxes; they were, of course, obliged to do so if they wanted the Irish government as their tenants! But Katie and Jim went well beyond the minimum to make us feel comfortable and happy as tenants; nicer people for landlords you could not find.

Others were less fortunate, and I ended up spending quite a lot of my time consoling Irish investors in Lithuania who lost out to unscrupulous locals and the vagaries of contract law and a legal system inherited, largely unchanged, from the communist regime (this was before the crash of 2008 which largely wiped out all investment activity from Ireland).

So every time I showed my card, the invariable response would be one of shock and awe. 'How, Ambassador, did you manage to find such an iconic location? I was there in 1989...' Some diplomatic colleagues may have had bigger, better and nicer offices (the Finns were located in a former KGB building) but none had the equal of our address which brought instant recognition and opened many conversational doors.

The local Diplomatic List is an all-important determinant of diplomatic life on a posting. The clock starts as soon as one arrives en poste though the official placement on the list is dated from the official presentation of credentials to the Head of State. One's placing on the list determines seniority among colleagues, and movement up the list is a jealously guarded tradition, determining such important matters as where one stands in the relatively long line to greet the president at his National Day reception, and who will be 'Dean' of the Diplomatic Corps, an 'onerous' office which involves even more invitations, attendance at national functions, for example when a Head of State visits, and general liaison with colleagues as boss of the Corps. In countries which recognise the Holy See the resident Nuncio is automatically the Dean of the Corps.

And we all vied to get as close to the top of the Diplomatic List as possible, a friendly rivalry unless any colleague chose to ignore their position.

In Lithuania we had a jolly, rotund German Archbishop as our Dean. Peter gave wonderful farewell parties, always going to great pains with his remarks to say flattering – and even sometimes barbed but apposite – comments about the departing colleague. He was quite a wit in his time. We attended many National Day receptions together over my five years in Vilnius, and what better way to while away a cold, dark evening than in good company with some local vodka shots on arrival to warm us up, a charming and civilised custom. I usually sought him out and he wasn't hard to find, bright puce sash around an ample tummy and gales of laughter around the social hub he generated. I recall him saying on one occasion,

> Donal, you remember the story of Jesus and the prostitute? The Good Lord stares hard at the menacing crowd surrounding the prostitute and says, 'Let those of you without sin cast the first stone!' With barely a pause, a small pebble whizzes by Jesus's ear… Jesus turns around in astonishment and says, 'Oh, Mother!'

Having waited a number of weeks, I eventually presented my credentials to President Adamkus in the Presidential Palace which is in the heart of the Old Town; the edifice was the former Governor-General's residence under eighteenth century Russian Imperial rule and can bear comparative scrutiny with our own President's residence, Áras an Uachtaráin. His welcome was also generous and hospitable in an Irish sense and he always found time for a few words whenever we met subsequently. He had been a mid-level employee of the US Environmental Protection Agency in Chicago for many years, and represented not only the country but a significant cohort of Lithuanian Americans who had rigorously maintained their culture, language and traditions while 'in exile' in the US, mostly in and around Illinois, and who had returned en masse after the fall of the communist regime.

Distinctive from those who had stayed and endured the 50 years' rule, their knowledge of the Lithuanian language was both archaic and formal, the result of many years of Saturday school abroad with no updating from its source. Likewise, they tended to stick together and to eschew what they considered to be the blinkered, narrow-minded nationalists who had remained behind. While they shared an agenda to push forward Lithuanian membership of (a) NATO, always the first national priority for the Baltics, especially so for Estonia and Lithuania and (b) the EU, where they were united in their determination that communist, socialist and populist movements were prevented from achieving political power in the country. But on a social level, they were as segregated as any two groups could be.

An example in practice was the character and manner of the two Presidents I knew while in Lithuania. The office of President of Lithuania is closely modelled on the US without any of the checks and balances which that country has in place. The president to whom I presented credentials was Adamkus from Chicago; he was both modest and pleasant. His successor as president in 2009 was Dalia Grybauskaite, known in the media as 'The Steel Magnolia' from her time in Brussels as a European Commissioner. She was Lithuanian-born in the Soviet era.

I had the privilege to escort her to Ireland for an official visit shortly after her election as president. With no small talk and a quiet manner, she was challenging, and clearly uncomfortable with our rather casual ways of meeting and greeting VIPs. Her main focus was on canvassing among the relatively large Lithuanian population in Ireland.

There was a myth, hard to correct, that Lithuania had lost hundreds of thousands of its best and brightest to the UK and to Ireland. Certainly, in Ireland, as our census of the period proved, there were several thousand who had emigrated after 1989 and, indeed, continued to do so, but nothing like the statistically un-substantiated figures mentioned in the local media, always a niggling disagreement between us. It was all part of the 'Polish plumber' syndrome prevalent in European media circles and of little enduring consequence.

Another story involving Lithuanians in Ireland comes to mind – my media arm-wrestle with the Ombudsman (a wom-an, as it happened) for Lithuanians Living Abroad. Known for her desire for publicity, she spoke to a journalist on a flight back from her first visit to Ireland and told him that she had received complaints from parents of Lithuanian children at school in Ire-land. Apparently, they had said that their offspring were being discriminated against by teachers and other children as 'Lithua-nian children are renowned for their good looks and Irish people resented this'! What rubbish. But the journalist had got his scoop.

Fortunately, I was tipped off by my 'practically-perfect-in-every-way' Embassy Secretary, Milda Joksaité, that the story was breaking news on a local web portal and trending on social media, still in its infancy. Realising that if I didn't nip this in the bud it would grow legs, I immediately informed HQ and issued a short statement saying I was both puzzled and disappointed by the allegations made by the Ombudsman, that nothing had been said before this, but that if such discrimination was occurring, which I doubted, I would be happy to review the evidence and to report it to the authorities. I also asked to meet with the Om-budsman as soon as possible.

This took the wind out of her sails and the media quickly lost interest. My subsequent meeting with her confirmed that she had absolutely no evidence to support her claims. I issued a further statement saying we had had a frank and constructive conversation and that she had agreed she would, in future, as a normal courtesy, liaise in advance with the Embassy of any concerns she had before talking to the media. Enough said!

About a year or so into the establishment of resident relations, a team from Dublin came on an inspection visit. Convention has it that when the team arrives anywhere, it is met by the local diplomat with the hallowed greeting, 'We are delighted to see you!' (No!) and the response from the visitors is, 'We are here to help' (No again!).

It took up our time for many weeks before the visit to ensure all was in order and that there would be no unpleasant surprises. The visit went well, and we got an A1 rating which was both pleasing and a relief. The only wobble was that I had arranged to take the team out for a meal the night before they left, during which they were to give me an informal account of the report which they would make to our Management Committee on re-turn.

I went early to the chosen venue to ensure the table location was suitable and so on – diplomats are like scouts, always pre-pared! To my horror, I discovered that the restaurant had with-out advance notice given their entire dining room over to a party hosted by a Lithuanian Government Minister! Not even stopping to protest at this outrage, I dashed out the door and down the road to the SAS Hotel dining room and grabbed a table. I then dashed out the door again and managed to 'bump into' my in-spector colleagues just as they appeared at the end of the street in question. Saying nothing, I diverted them to the hotel table and we had a pleasant and uneventful meal as if the entire scenario had been planned accordingly. I never told them of the potential calamity that presented itself earlier in the evening. As Charles Dickens wrote in *Great Expecations*, 'On the Rampage, Pip, and off the Rampage, Pip – such is Life!'

As the two incidents above indicate, Lithuanians may not be known for their communications skills or for forward planning.

The official high point of my time as Ambassador – there were many wonderful experiences – was the State Visit by President Mary McAleese in early summer, 2007, just before the Irish General Election of that year in which Bertie Ahern won a handsome victory. Mary Mac is everyone's favourite aunty and her ever-supportive spouse, Martin, is one of nature's gentlemen. A nicer couple one could not meet and a dream to work for on State occasions. She has such a healing personality, in contrast to the much more formal demeanour of her predecessor in that office.

I was the note-taker at her conversation with President Adamkus and she was brilliant! She spoke so eloquently, and her counterpart did as well, each learning from the other. Adamkus wanted to know all about the Celtic Tiger economy that the international media banged on about; how could Lithuania repeat our success? What was the secret? Mary's response was frank and unexpected: learn from our mistakes, not our achievements. How right she was proven. Fortunately, Lithuania was a good pupil and did avoid our excesses and errors. The Lithuanian economy is doing fine, and many of the Lithuanians who emigrated to Ireland in the 1990s and early 2000s are now prospering back at home.

The conversation between the two presidents ran on for so long that the Chief of Protocol had to interrupt to remind his boss that our president had a press conference to attend and that the media were already gathered downstairs. Adamkus turned to Mary and asked, 'What is the difference between a protocol officer and a terrorist?' Pausing a bit, he then offered, 'One can negotiate with a terrorist!' A good rapport had been cemented and had set the positive and relaxed tone for the remainder of her visit.

On a hot afternoon of the second day and with an hour or so downtime between the tightly sequenced programme of events, Mary asked if I would take her on a short tour of some of the Old Town. Somebody had told her that I gave good customised walking tours and, indeed, it was something I enjoyed doing with visitors. In fact, a popular local magazine, *Lithuania Now*, subsequently featured an article about my tours.

So we set off to some haunts I liked to show to visitors. Along the way, President McAleese, who had in tow Martin and her Irish and Lithuanian security detail, suggested we stop for an ice cream. I knew the best place in town, deep in the narrow laneways of Old Town, on a corner, the perfect setting to sit and lick our cones. A tranquil scene, with the presidental couple and Siobhán and myself surrounded by suited bodyguards, was brutally interrupted by a throaty roar and plumes of oily smoke as a local Harley-Davidson rider sailed past. Quick as a wink, Mary turned to Pat, her Irish Garda Inspector shadow, and said, 'Pat, isn't that why we allow you to carry a weapon?' It was a visit to remember!

I also had the pleasure of descending into the bowels of the earth to view the inside of an intercontinental ballistic missile

(ICBM) silo. The opportunity came about as a result of a tip-off from my British colleague, like myself an inveterate history enthusiast and frequent explorer of the lesser known parts of Lithuania. Thanks to the initiative shown by the local tourist board, who had realised the potential of such a hidden treasure in their midst, the silo complex, abandoned in a hurry by the Russians in 1990, had lain largely undisturbed ever since. It exists in a spectacularly beautiful, relatively remote part of northeastern Lithuania, far from any major conurbations, which was why it was chosen as a top-secret ICBM site in the first place.

As explained to us by our guide, the base consisted of an entire army barracks, with residential accommodation for a battalion of Soviet troops, engineers, maintenance crews and so on, even down to a small village of shops to make the base virtually self-sufficient. Moscow had brought in several thousand construction workers from Estonia in 1960 to build it and then shipped them back again to preserve its secrecy.

Rusting barbed wire, water puddles and a dank concrete bunker announced that we had reached the core of the site, the vast silo extending deep underground. The surface cone of the six missile tubes was disguised and later overgrown by shrubbery and vegetation, merging them seamlessly.

A seemingly endless warren of stairs and sloping corridors brought us to the epicentre, the control room and the main shaft of one of the missiles. Much was as the Soviets had left it: stark grey concrete, naked light bulbs and water dripping eerily down walls and from ceilings. Ubiquitous nuclear warning signs abounded, as did complicated looking switch boards and maps of the world with capital cities clearly marked. When loaded into their cavernous firing shafts in 1962 and for a couple of decades beyond, these six ICBM missiles were trained on the West and could have been launched at a moment's notice.

Fortunately, history proved benign and we were spared the worst threat of the Cold War. But it did bring home in stark terms the very real fear engendered, for example, during the Cuban Missile Crisis of 1962; peering precariously over the ledge at the top of the missile shaft, one appreciated the massive scale of these lethal weapons.

I was told that several deaths had occurred since the Soviets had left the site, mainly those of local fortune hunters who had robbed the facility of its generators and other practical, reusable equipment, but that otherwise most of the facility was untouched since it fell into disuse abruptly in 1989. The missiles themselves were displaced and transferred across the Russian border where they presumably met a peaceful fate on the nuclear scrapheap.

I am also pleased to say that I played a role in the closure of Ignalina, Lithuania's only Soviet-era nuclear reactor. Together with my EU colleagues, we put local pressure on the government to live up to its commitment given to Brussels prior to EU membership, to phase out and close down what was Chernobyl-like reactor technology. While Lithuania claimed that their reactor was much better maintained and operated much stricter safety precautions than its misfortunate Ukrainian counterpart, the fact remained that Ignalina had no failsafe mechanism and that a disaster similar to that which had occurred in Reactor No. 4 at Chernobyl on 26 April 1986 could occur again.

It was obvious to me when I arrived in Vilnius that the Lithuanian Government was prevaricating about a closure date. Ignalina provided in excess of 80 per cent of the country's electricity generation needs and did so cheaply. Not only did the 2,000 or so ethnic Russian employees of Ignalina receive free electricity for their domestic needs (rumour had it that it was also a bribe to suppress any health concerns about living close by), but the whole country benefited from well below market energy prices by European standards. So it wasn't proving easy for any Lithuanian government to accept closure.

It took a lot of both honey and vinegar, but the government finally complied, a date was given for closure which was adhered to by and large. It did throw up the challenge of quickly finding alternative energy sources and the temporary redundancy of a large number of skilled workers, but it had to be done for the greater good. I do not regret being an activist in that cause. Talking of Chernobyl...

And Belarus

Early on in my posting I became aware that the Finnish Ambassador had a secondary, that is, non-residential, accreditation to Belarus (translated as white Russia of old, *biel* being the Russian word for white). He regaled EU meetings with his tales from almost weekly visits across the iron border between Lithuania and Belarus. Vilnius is only 20 kilometres from the border crossing and Minsk is another 100 kilometres down a dead-straight dual carriageway. His accounts of his visits to Minsk intrigued me.

I mentioned my curiosity to the Swedish No. 2; their Vilnius Embassy was also accredited and he, too, was a frequent visitor. He immediately offered to take me on one of his trips, a day out in Minsk to introduce me to the city itself and to members of the artistic community there, with whom he had built up close friendships. I jumped at the opportunity. Mind you, as I had learnt long ago, and which Mary Robinson was fond of quoting, 'seek forgiveness, not permission', so I only told Dublin after the event of my visit beyond the fringe.

And what a revelation it was. Bypassing the articulated trucks backed up for kilometres on the Lithuanian side, we sailed through the immigration and customs formalities. My first surprise was that the Belarussian border officers, who included some very attractive females, were much more welcoming than their sulky Lithuanian counterparts.

The road to Minsk was a joy to drive, straight, two lanes, with little traffic, since the truckies rested up after their border ordeal, preferring to travel by night when the cover of darkness gave them some anonymity. It took just over an hour to cover the 100 kilometres to the outskirts of what proved to be a major conurbation. I fell in love with Minsk at first sight!

Minsk was largely razed to the ground during the Great Patriotic War, that is, World War II, in some of the fiercest fighting of the German Eastern Campaign, up there with Leningrad and Stalingrad in terms of devastation. Like those two iconic battlefields, Minsk was awarded the select status of 'Hero City' by Stalin after the war ended, one of only five, I believe, to carry that title. And it is, as a consequence, one of the finest examples of what can be called Stalinist architecture, densely packed suburbs of residential tower blocks, row upon row as far as the eye can see and new ones being added in a constantly widening girdle. This petticoat style may not appeal to everyone's design taste, but it works, in context, as an effective way to provide decent, modest shelter quickly to those desperately in need of same after that terrible conflagration visited upon them across the land.

As one gets closer to the centre, the city becomes a spider web of broad boulevards, dominant square-shaped four-story buildings of largely uniform style though with discreet architectural flourishes, a subliminal flashback to an earlier period as anyone familiar with Georgian Dublin would immediately recognise. The same stylistic restrictions, including on height, also applied in Stalinist Minsk, coincidence or not. And then one notices that all the streets are pristine. Every morning just as the sun rises, an army of 'babushkas', elderly women, appear out of nowhere, brooms in hand, to begin the task of sweeping the pavements. Mind you, they don't have a lot of litter to pick up as everyone in the city is careful about their waste. Lots of green open spaces, formal parks for the most part – Minsk has its own Gorky Park, kindred to its Moscow counterpart and equally as popular with the locals – and water features abound. Yes, it may not be to everyone's taste, but I like it a lot.

One of Minsk's most famous twentieth century residents, though he isn't mentioned in local guide books, is one Lee Harvey Oswald. My Finnish friend was able to point to a rather elegant apartment building overlooking Gorky Park in which both Oswald and his beautiful Belarussian spouse, Marina, lived prior to his return to the States.

Oswald, a trained US Marine, visited the Soviet Union in 1959 on a holiday visa. He applied to remain, claiming he could supply secret information regarding the notorious U2 spy plane. Oswald was 'interviewed' in Moscow for a period before having his application rejected. When he cut his wrists on the day before he was due to leave, the KGB reconsidered. He was interrogated and found not to know anything of any great value but rather than send him home, he was given a sinecure job at a large radio manufacturer based in Minsk, then a rather remote part of the Soviet Empire.

Oswald is remembered as quite the party-goer in Minsk and, as one of very few foreigners living in the city, became quite the local celebrity. It was while in Minsk that he met and married Marina, an attractive local girl. What is difficult to explain is how he managed to return without prosecution to the USA in 1962, bringing Marina with him and, as we know, settling in the Dallas area. Some things never change, as we have seen from the recent spate of home-grown terrorist events.

Minsk also contains what I consider could be a future wonder of the world, a highly unusual isometric national library building which combines its formal function as a library with a national conference centre and a major tourist attraction and art gallery. With ever-changing lighting at night to rival the Eiffel Tower, it was, I was told, funded by a nationwide 'contribution', or individual tax, something only a dictator could successfully impose on the people.

Which brings me to President Alexander Lukashenko, often described, especially by Americans, as the Last Dictator in Europe. I believe that to be a rather simplistic, inaccurate description of someone who has shown great political mastery, guile and tenacity since he came to power in a fractured Belarus in 1994, some 26 years ago.

When I presented credentials at a modest ceremony the one and only time I met him, done in the Hall of the Heroes in honour of the fallen of the Great Patriotic War, he singled out the country's and his own personal gratitude to the Irish people for all they continued to do in the wake of the Chernobyl nuclear explosion (Chernobyl is in Ukraine but on the border with Belarus and the wind blew that week from the south).

That was my one and only encounter with the Charlie Chaplin of Eastern Europe. I did see KGB on every street corner and lots of military presence on public occasions.

During my first trip I was introduced to several members of the visual arts community who have remained firm friends. I returned to Vilnius much enthused by my initial visit behind the real, still very much in existence, Iron Curtain of Communism. I immediately set out a proposal to Dublin to take over the non-residential accreditation of Ireland in Belarus from my colleagues in Moscow. I argued that I was much closer in Vilnius and could achieve more as a result, both in political coverage of events there by attending weekly EU meetings and in terms of exploring potential economic and trade linkages. Moscow visited for a few days once a year, if they had the time and inclination, whereas I could be down and back in the same day which made for a more cost effective use of scarce resources. Most 'serious players' either had residential diplomatic missions in Minsk or covered it from Vilnius.

In a rare moment of sanity, the Department agreed with my arguments but with the proviso that the transfer should await a change of colleague as Ambassador in Moscow. This meant waiting a further two years before achieving official status as Irish Ambassador to Belarus.

In the meantime, I got active, taking advantage of all invitations to visit, often going to EU Heads of Mission meetings in Minsk as a guest of the local Ambassadors and in the company of my Finnish colleague, the late and much-lamented Timo Lahelma, who was religious in observing his own role as a visiting non-resident Ambassador.

The EU meetings were held in the large if not particularly lavish Embassy of France, which claimed to have as part of its facilities the only 'secure room' among EU embassies in Minsk. The secure room was, it turned out, a cramped, stuffy, dreary, windowless, lead-lined space – a bank vault without the money!

Mind you, not only was it physically uncomfortable and unpleasant, but some of the comments between colleagues were distinctly unedifying. Without disclosing State secrets, our host was cynical in the extreme. The Germans wanted nothing to change; the Brits wanted to change everything. The Poles wanted to go to war while the Italians, pusillanimous as ever, just wanted to trade. Berlusconi was a big friend of Lukashenka who made a rare visit westwards to Rome and hosted his Italian mate in return. The Spanish and the Dutch were literally not at the table, covering Belarus in theory either from Moscow or from Poland.

I recall that on one occasion, on leaving the French Embassy, I was tailed, none too subtly, all the way back to the Lithuanian border by Belarussian security forces. I waved farewell as they began to turn back.

On another visit, this time to an artist friend at his family's country dacha (a modest holiday retreat, deep in the forest, commonplace among the general Belarussian populace whose sanity was preserved by such places), I picked up a tail just after leaving their village. I don't know how they found me there but I suspect one of the neighbours was on the payroll to report any suspicious visitors. To throw them off the scent, we went on another detour to a larger town and visited the local art gallery. Later, when I asked my friend if he had had any follow-up visits from our KFGB friends he said 'no', so I believe our little subterfuge may have worked!

I waited impatiently for the two years to be up and once I heard the name of a new colleague being assigned to the Embassy in Moscow, I reminded Dublin of their commitment. They confirmed it and before you could cross the border I was calling on both my Belarussian and Finnish counterparts in Vilnius to tell them my good news. Both were delighted, the one to have closer, more practical links, and the other for the company!

It took some months to establish a date for the presentation of my official 'letters of credence' to President Lukashenko, the diplomatic formality process for new Ambassadors; I described this event earlier. I must add that any of the Belarussian Foreign Ministry diplomats I encountered could have graced the foreign ministry of any western country. They were suave, sophisticated and spoke beautiful English.

In the meantime, I was allowed to visit as if I was already accredited and so began fortnightly visits to Belarus. I notified all of the Irish Chernobyl NGOs active in Belarus and began a process of visiting their projects. Obviously, Adi Roche's Chernobyl Children's Project was the original and best-known and, indeed, I formed a close friendship with Adi over the years since the Oscar ceremony in 2003 (see San Francisco chapter), but I also made some new friends by contacting the other charities active in Belarus. These include Children of Chernobyl, Chernobyl Relief, and Chernobyl Children's Trust, all excellent Irish NGOs.

It was to be a rich vein for supporting their good work. For example, I was able to help the Chernobyl Children's Project with their annual summer and Christmas trips for Chernobyl children to Ireland by facilitating their transit through Vilnius and on to direct flights to Dublin, rather than being forced to travel via London or to hire charter flights. And I provided an official bridge for them all with local and national Belarussian bureaucracy, making a point of calling upon local officialdom and keeping the relevant Ministry in Minsk fully informed. This led, on one notable occasion, to having to apply considerable pressure on a local authority to cough up their part of a bargain with CCP to build a new care centre, in part financed by Irish government funding. Adi Roche was most grateful for my intervention.

On the trade front, I had mixed success. In order to get the ball rolling – and not much had happened in the previous era during Embassy Moscow coverage – I began to plan for a small trade mission from Ireland, with the help of the nearest EI office. Ironically, that, too, was Moscow-centred but I found a willing ally in their active representative at the time. I don't, by the way, mean to criticise my former colleagues in Moscow; it was no one's fault that their official jurisdiction, Russia and much of the former Soviet Union, was a vast territory to cover with an extremely small staff. I did suggest later that one way of providing more effective cover would be, again, to follow the Finnish example by creating a dedicated roving Ambassador to cover the 'Stans', five major constituencies in the Soviet Empire. Alas, as on so many other issues, I am still awaiting a response!

To note: when Irish bureaucracy, civil, public and not least local, is posed a challenging question, or one that focuses on a weakness in the system, the invariable default position is to freeze and do nothing, hoping the questioner will give up. In this, it resembles the primeval adrenalin reaction to fight, freeze or flee with the middle one being the safest option.

I led a smallish trade mission of 10 or so companies to Minsk where we engaged in rather sterile, formal talks reminiscent of

the Soviet era (their suggestion) and one-on-one company sessions (our suggestion). This format seemed to work well and
there were a number of follow-up contacts which led to some
new economic activity.

However, the problems we faced were two-fold: the Belarussians could not take any final decision on anything without
referring it to 'The President's Office', a relatively small group
of close-knit and trusted advisors with whom Lukashenka had
surrounded himself. Lukashenka rotated this cohort into and out
of the more sensitive ministries and positions, such as Cabinet
Office Secretary, the Justice Ministry, Chief of the KGB and Head
of the Army. All other ministries were basically jobs for the boys
but without any influence on centralised decision-making. So
we faced inertia when it came to cooperation and turning it into
something tangible.

The second problem is that the infamous Icelandic ash cloud
eruption distracted everyone on the final day with the flight to
London suspended and everyone making frantic attempts to
get home by alternative means; the untamed power of nature at
work! I ended up facilitating an extended, forced stopover for
three of the Irish members of our trade delegation, and one has
since become a good friend, Denis Parfenov.

The trade mission led to further talks, for example on a possible takeover of the running of Belarussian duty free shops, offered by Aer Rianta International (ARI). Belarus had a chain of
lucrative duty free shops strategically placed along its borders
and at the airport in Minsk, as well as a diplomats-only facility in
the city centre. ARI offered potential expansion of this business
and financial benefits, as per their extremely positive experience
at that time in running Russian duty free facilities.

Alas, it was not to be. Despite convincing our senior Belarussian interlocutor, the Head of Aviation Services, that it would be a win-win for them, he was too nervous of putting his head over the presidential office parapet to seek sanction. Obviously, the fear of incurring the wrath of the president for taking an initiative involving any risk, no matter how remote, outweighed the potential gains from a successful deal, both for the State and for the president. So he prevaricated and held on to his position a while longer and we walked away frustrated. ARI were beginning to develop China's markets at the time so Belarus was relatively insignificant.

At a later date, Irish Cement tried to take on the running of the Grodno Cement works; again, their efforts were met with obfuscation and delay. Such were the perils facing those who were in any way interested in doing business in Belarus.

One of the most rewarding aspects of visiting Belarus was to witness the good work being carried out by our Chernobyl charities. The herculean efforts of Adi Roche, a living saint if ever there was one, driven beyond her normal endurance to improve the health and quality of life of neglected children in Belarus, deserves a book in itself. Her initiative spawned several other Irish-founded organisations that, in their own way, also made an enormous contribution in Belarus including one, as mentioned above, that President Lukashenka himself acknowledged. If nothing else, his support for our collective national efforts on Chernobyl was genuine and we should respect him for that, at least.

It was interesting to observe that what began as a simple desire to help children who were victims of the nuclear reactor explosion widened out considerably by Adi and others. Belarus, in common with other former Soviet Bloc States, operated a policy of taking children born with congenital physical and mental conditions from their family environments and placing them in often remote, institutional orphanages; shades of a Magdalene Laundry approach to the mentally and physically challenged.

Thus, many of the children who benefitted from our Chernobyl-inspired concern were not, in fact, directly or even indirectly affected by nuclear fall-out, but had been institutionalised by the State as a way of dealing with nature's abnormalities. This nuance is, perhaps, not made entirely transparent by our Chernobyl NGO community, understandably so, given the competitive nature of their fundraising efforts. Still, they perform a vital kindness which the State fails to execute in relation to the most vulnerable and neglected in that poverty-stricken society.

At the other end of the spectrum, those young Belarussians bright enough to aspire to third-level education have a small but reasonably high quality academic institutions from which to choose. And one of these has a rather unique profile and background, namely the European Humanities University (EHU).

I came across EHU in September, 2005, as a result of exchanging visiting cards with its Provost, Dr. Anatoli Mikhailov, during a National Day function, one of the first such occasions I attended after my arrival in Vilnius.

A small but important digression: visiting cards may be an archaic and seemingly expensive habit, but for me they have generated immense added-value over my 42 years of handing them out like confetti, as we say. Our distinctive, elegant official gold harp on the visiting card has been a constant source of conversation and a great door-opener around the world. My assertion that Ireland is the only country in the world that has a musical instrument as its national emblem has never been contradicted, though many have tried! I often added, for provocative value, that it showed the peaceful and cultured nature of our society!

Exchanging cards is also an efficient and discreet way of finding out how your interlocutor spells their name, their title and where to find them without labouring the point. Visiting cards provide a mini-surface for writing notes and other personal details and, not least, for disengaging from conversations when necessary, for example, 'Must dash, here's my card; give me a call sometime ... bye!'

In sum, they are a useful diplomatic tool, essential to plying our trade effectively.

So, I took Anatoli up on an invitation to visit EHU, more out of curiosity than with any agenda in mind. I had, moreover, already decided that in my first year in Lithuania, as I had practiced elsewhere, I would take up every invitation that came my way. Only later would I become more discerning in my scheduling.

I found myself walking down a long alleyway to an old building hidden away behind a main Vilnius thoroughfare convenient to downtown and not far from the Lithuanian Ministry of Foreign Affairs. It turned out that EHU had been established by Mikhailov and a few academic friends as a private university in Minsk in 1994, shortly after the creation of Belarus from the remains of the Soviet Union. It had thrived in its early years, boasting many of the children of the regime as students and graduates, but had slowly become a centre of political dissent as Lukashenko revealed increasingly dictatorial tendencies. The final bust-up occurred in 2004 when a Presidential decree ordered closure of the Minsk campus.

Ever keen to rattle the communist dictator's cage, and to give the proverbial two fingers to Moscow, the Lithuanian government stepped into the breach and offered EHU asylum in Vilnius. I am still unconvinced that the Lithuanians had anticipated that Mikhailov would gladly accept their offer, or had worked out the enormous resource implications their kindness generated, but that is what happened!

EHU 2

I was one of the early supporters of this 'university in exile' as it quickly became known. I managed to convince my colleagues in the Irish Aid division to provide some modest grants to support existing EHU programmes. EHU became the flavour of the day with the European Commission, with the Nordic Council of Ministers and with a group of ideologically-driven US foundations who were awash with State Department funds. Other EU colleagues followed my lead as well.

But, as was typical of third-level academic institutions, the political in-fighting among staff was truly vicious. Academics could teach our politicians a thing or two when it comes to that particular blood sport! EHU was riven by many factions and also riddled with Lukashenko spies and saboteurs. There was a distinct fault line between those conservatives who saw the move across the border to Lithuania as a 'temporary little arrangement' pending reconciliation with Minsk, and those progressives who wanted to drop the 'university in exile' label and to adapt to its new EU environment as quickly as possible.

I tried to steer a course somewhere in between, supporting attempts to make EHU as self-sufficient as possible (that is, generating revenue) while at the same time retaining close connections with Belarus with a view to being ready one day to return to a free and democratic society with an exciting future. To that end, I sought to promote the idea of a Business School within the university which would offer an Executive MBA programme. Once established, that programme could generate an income stream and be a source of revenue for the university itself.

Despite many twist and turns, and with modest help from the Kemmy Business School at University of Limerick, Irish Aid funded a three-year pilot programme which turned into a fully-fledged, profit-making operation for EHU. This was thanks largely to the unstinting efforts of the Business Programme Director, Pavel Malukovich. 'Little Paul', as he was affectionately known, despite his considerable bulk and large frame, became a close ally in the continual struggle against the forces of inertia in EHU's governing echelons who preferred not to sully their traditional academic record. Good sense prevailed and the Business Programme took off and lasted a good ten years.

Many students and staff were sufficiently motivated to make the best of their precarious continuous existence in Vilnius, many making a weekly commute from their homes in Belarus, coping with long and frustrating, sometimes personally perilous, border-crossings, while others gave up their relatively comfortable existence in Belarus for a more modest lifestyle on the outskirts of Vilnius. Both students and staff did so in the belief that they were destined to provide a cadre of educated young people who would be ready to step up to the mark when Lukashenko and his regime finally toppled.

I still hope that they will and that in my own personal commitment to EHU I have played a small part, a footnote in the history books, in nudging Belarus forward into the twenty-first century.

On a personal level, one of the sadder episodes of life in Lithuania was the news received in early 2006 that my sister Triona, a chemo nurse in Somerset, had herself been diagnosed with oesophageal cancer, stage 4. She was so brave, but it was at an advanced stage by the time her treatment started.

Undeterred, Triona came to visit us accompanied by her husband Ian, a self-taught computer whiz, and my nephew Jon. Triona had three children, my niece, Sinead, who I am proud to say is a police officer in Somerset; Jon, a gifted academic researcher working in London, with whom I have the most interesting political conservations; and his loveable brother, the rascally rogue of the family, Jamie, who is living and working in New Zealand, but hopefully not forever!

As a present, we sent her up in one of the hot air balloons for which Vilnius is justly famous and of which she had no fear! Prudence, if not downright cowardice, prevented me from accompanying her and I am now sorry I did not do so! Her visit was filled with happiness and fond memories, despite the looming cloud hanging over us.

Less than a year later, Triona was dead, a painful and utterly desolate end for someone who lit up our lives on so many occasions, who did much good for many and no harm to any.

My time in Vilnius came to a reluctant end in summer 2010. My posting had been extended by one year and HQ were diligent in wanting me to move home for a period, having last served there in 2001, and even then I had been on secondment to Kildare Street. My last posting before that in Iveagh House had been in 1990-1993!

It was a profound shock to the system to be going home, but I hoped I had built up enough credit to be able to influence those in authority where I might serve at HQ. No such luck! I sent in my preferences, stating clearly that the one place I particularly did not want to end up was EU Division. And several heated conversations later, I was assigned … to the EU Division.

When asked which of the foreign postings I enjoyed the most, my invariable answer has been that I have 'enjoyed' them all, but if pressed, I must say that Lithuania was among the very best!

Our Seventh EU Presidency

I knew in advance it would mean that at least three of my five final years would be spent at home, something I did not particularly look forward to, facing the prospect of retirement without a further foreign posting.

It was also a difficult time to be home with the country plunged into a prolonged period of uninvited austerity imposed by Brussels, the IMF and, indeed, the US whose Treasury Secretary, Larry Summers, refused to let our Government share the misery with our banking sector's investors, many of whom were US hedge funds. People were understandably angry and the public service and our politicians were taking the brunt of media criticism.

I am assuming most readers will have their own direct recollections of this awful time so I will focus on just a few memories which I regard as significant.

Shortly after the Fine Gael–Labour coalition came to power, Lucinda Creighton instituted preparations for our June 2013 EU Presidency, my seventh. As one of her initiatives, it was announced on 12 July 2011, without any prior warning, that two-thirds of what was then the DFA's European Union Division would move to the Taoiseach's Department, under Lucinda's control and with a new Assistant Secretary in charge, the politically astute Geraldine Byrne Nason.

Our own Assistant Secretary, Peter Gunning, who knew more than anyone else about the EU (he had served as No. 2 in Brussels for several years) was disappointed, to say the least. Peter departed shortly after the announcement as our Representative to the Council of Europe.

Lucinda Creighton, I discovered, was a joy to work with. She listened and encouraged, and she ran a vigorous presidency. Lucinda and her colleagues made the neglected countries of Eastern Europe, Moldova, Ukraine and Georgia, as priority targets to foster a more cooperative attitude towards the EU. Under our presidency, we brought them much closer to Brussels. I was pleased that she took on one of my protégés, Shane Cahill, as her Private Secretary to Minister of State (PSMS), on my recommendation. And her Special Advisor, Stephen O'Shea, was brilliant to work with too, rare enough for the cohort of unelected political advisors who are the real rulers of our political class.

Alas, within a year, the entire scene had changed and Russia was at odds with Brussels. I believe that the Germans and the Dutch played less than fair in EU internal discussions, closely supported by the French. Internal dissention as much as external animosities caused the Ukraine debacle.

In the meantime, shortly after what was generally recognised to be a good, if not spectacular, presidency, Lucinda astounded everyone by not having a Plan B when it came to her disagreement with the Fine Gael party line on abortion. Her dismissal by Taoiseach Enda Kenny, seemingly a big fan of Lucinda, was a serious blow to the government and to our credibility in Europe. She had in her relatively brief time as EU Minister built up a wide web of friendships across the continent, in particular through her role as Vice President of the European People's Party (EPP) and through her conscientious attention to the European Parliament during our presidency.

One of the most interesting eruptions during this period at HQ was the headline-making closure of one of our oldest diplomatic missions, our Embassy to The Holy See, located in one of our finest State-owned properties, the Villa Spada. The Villa was subsequently sequestered as the new residence of our Ambassador to Italy, a smart move.

Our Vatican Embassy had been an important listening post during World War II (see Dermot Keogh's excellent history thereof) but had declined in status since EU membership in 1973. The break in diplomatic relations was dramatically underlined by, in my humble opinion, an intemperate Dáil speech by Enda Kenny who blamed the Roman Curia for the child abuse cover-up scandals which racked Irish society.

Ironically, our DFA Secretary General was David Cooney who had only recently returned from being 'Our Man in the Vatican' to take up the top post. It was exceptionally difficult for him to accept this particular closure, especially as the official excuse, which nobody seriously entertained, was 'for economic reasons'. The closure was given a further fig leaf of credibility by closing our mission to Iran at the same time, though again this was a short-term saving at the expense of our long-term reputation in that region.

My HQ Section in the Europe Division was responsible for Western Europe bilateral relations and the Vatican Closure file was plonked on my desk. David monitored our output closely; everything had to be cleared through his office. A postcard campaign, which meant a confetti blizzard of cards arriving on a daily basis from those opposing the closure, was likewise ignored. A personal letter from a former Secretary General and high-profile Fine Gael supporter offering to mediate was also spurned. A Vatican initiative to send a more personable representative to Dublin in the person of Charlie Brown, a relatively young US priest, had no effect.

We were told we would have to wait two years before any move was made to repair the relationship; and, indeed, so it proved. In my humble opinion, we should not have taken the decision to close, which did not achieve any significant savings in the longer term or as a percentage of overall departmental expenditure, but which caused a deep and enduring rift in relations with the Roman Catholic hierarchy.

During this period, I found myself having my own serious doubts about EU enlargement policy. The revelation that Turkey was being paid over 500 million euros per annum – half a billion! – just to sit in the EU membership waiting room, and that this had been going on for decades, led to my total and absolute disillusionment with such initiatives. Moreover, it was increasingly obvious that Franco-German hegemony was going to become the norm when it came to the EU's future decision-making and direction. And that was well before Brexit became a reality!

I also applied for a post in the new European External Action Service. I was one of three who got a one-on-one interview with EEA Head and Commission VP Catherine Ashton, and I am pleased that she put my name forward as one of three candidates for the post of Deputy Head of Mission at the EU Embassy to the US in DC. Much to my personal disappointment, I got little enough support from my own Department and the post went to the French candidate whose country had actively lobbied in his favour, as the French always do. It was, yet again for Ireland, an opportunity missed to have someone in a useful international position.

So, I was ready to move again.

For once, my luck held. In fact, my efforts during our presidency, in particular as our last-minute step-in representative on the Eastern Europe group in Brussels (due to the sudden illness of a colleague in the Mission there) which involved many trips to my least favourite European city, were, it seemed, appreciated. I was offered the post of Ambassador to Finland in early 2013.

I effected what was probably the quickest transfer from HQ to a foreign posting in the annals of the DFA, helped by the fact that my predecessor in Finland had decided to retire early rather than take a home posting.

Chapter 9

Helsinki

Finland, Finland, Finland
The country where I quite want to be
Your mountains so lofty
Your treetops so tall
Finland, Finland, Finland
Finland has it all

– 'Finland', by Monty Python

This final chapter might have been shorter, as when I went to Helsinki I knew I had only two years and one month of my working life as a civil servant left. It was with intent and purpose that I arrived in beautiful Helsinki. I would try my best to accomplish in two years a profile for Ireland that would normally take the full four or five years of a normal ambassadorial posting. I could have sat back, as some colleagues would be tempted to do, and spend all my time in Helsinki, enjoying the social and diplomatic rounds. But Helsinki is not the Dublin of Ireland; it has a relatively small share of the national population spread – 10 per cent – with eight to ten conurbations of importance spread across the extensive length of the country.

Instead, I did a whirlwind tour on as many of the eighty or so ambassadorial colleagues as I could meet in as short a time as possible; that is diplomatic protocol. With the knowledge I gleaned from their experiences, I drew up a simple, ultimately quite effective plan of campaign. I would visit a city or regional centre outside of Helsinki every six weeks or so, following my own trusted pattern of calls on local politicians and officials, meetings with the local Chamber of Commerce network (and as many of their SME members as I could pull together) and a visit to the local third-level campus. And I used excellent Finnish public transport, the national train network, for the most part to do so.

Finland has over sixteen universities and over twenty institutes of technology, a rich motherlode of research and development which I discovered had close academic ties with their Irish equivalents. This strategy, I am pleased to report, worked well and gave me an extensive range of business and cultural contacts in a relatively short space of time. Indeed, the Irish State agencies, IDA, Enterprise Ireland, Bord Bia and so on all began to notice my reports and started to turn up in Helsinki – which was a gratifying acknowledgement that I was making a difference in a hitherto neglected, low priority market for them. Armed with my narrative of similarities and opportunities, I set off on a short but epic adventure that saw me visit Lapland in the north, inside the Arctic Circle, and yes, I did unearth at least one Irish resident there, to Imatra on the eastern border, where Hitler once landed for a brief visit to Mannerheim in 1943, to the Aaland islands in the western Baltic, consisting mainly of Swedish-speaking people but under Finnish rule.

Again, I was struck by the geography and historic similarities between our two nations. Finland is in the far north, with a large segment of Lapland inside the Arctic Circle, and is, as I used to say, 'on the eastern edge of empire', meaning the modern equivalent of the ancient Roman empire. I liked to draw on the analogy from the film *A Few Good Men* of being 'on the wall'. I suppose I had also been reading too many *Game of Thrones* novels!

But one is aware that Finland is a small country with a large neighbour to the east – in this case, Masha, the Russian Bear – just as we are. Like Ireland, Finland is an old nation but a new country. It gained its independence in 1917; we started in 1916 and achieved our independence in 1922. The Finns fought each other immediately thereafter, as we did. Looking back a bit further, both Finland and Ireland had great famines in the mid-nineteenth century.

We have both gained a population of five plus million, though their age profile reflects a much older cohort share. Both Finland and Ireland have two national languages; in their case, approximately 12 per cent are Swedish-speaking Finns.

And building on these well-known comparisons, I used to remind my audiences that both countries have an excellent UN peacekeeping record, most recently through our joint Finnish-Irish Battalion in the Lebanon and in close collaboration in such areas as Human Rights and Humanitarian Affairs. Likewise, we both have long-established traditions of military neutrality, though this tends to be more politically controversial in Finland. There is a significant minority who support NATO membership – probably a majority of their armed forces do so. Thus, while ostensibly neutral, Finland participates in regional

NATO exercises and Helsinki is on the list of frequently visited ports by NATO naval squadrons.

The one time foreign minister, Timo Soini (2015-2019), leader of the populist right-wing Finns Party, had close Irish connections. He spoke fondly of visiting Ireland to learn English, staying with an Irish family in the southwest, near Tralee I believe.

It was during one of his visits that he converted from Lutheranism to Roman Catholicism, not necessarily a popular thing to do. There are only 5,000 or so Finnish Catholics out of five million inhabitants. Timo thought highly of all things Irish and had been Chair of the Friends of Ireland National Assembly group. Ironically, Soini is an avid Millwall F.C. supporter, flying to East London to watch home games; not only had he poor taste in soccer clubs but he may find it more difficult to attend home games following Brexit!

Finland also uses nuclear energy and has little difficulty with that stance. It also has a thriving arms industry, with no moral qualms about that either. But no country is perfect, eh?

What Finland does have, in spades, is a beautiful coastline, lots of lakes, lots of trees and lovely people. It can be a harsh climate but the Finnish lifestyle, using nature's gifts, compensates accordingly.

And Finns love their sauna. One of the first people to approach me on arrival in Helsinki was the president of the Sauna Society. He actually offered me a free membership for the first year and unlimited use of their facilities during that period to all incoming ambassadors, a clever marketing ploy. I wasn't in a rush, being Irish and therefore a bit shy of being naked in front of others (though Lithuania, which also likes its sauna parties, had over time lessened my hang-up on that score).

In Helsinki, there was no resident Vatican representative so it was the longest-serving ambassador who inherited both the title and role of Dean of the Diplomatic Corps, in this case, the Russian Ambassador of nine years standing, a genial former Minister for Nuclear Energy, a subject on which he waxed eloquent when allowed. In any event, the Danish Ambassador was a fine lady who had arrived one place ahead of me on that all-important Diplomatic List, as described earlier. So it was that she got her invitation to the sauna ahead of me. She went on about how wonderful it was, and how brave she was to immerse herself in the freezing lake water beside the sauna – the end of the ritual – so much that I was determined not to shirk it when my turn came to be invited.

I set off one evening to meet the male members of the Finnish Sauna Society. Yes, alas, in Finland saunas are strictly segregated, a bit like Irish golf clubs, with separate evenings for each sex. It is presumably their Lutheran upbringing, of which more anon; the Lithuanians are not so prudish. All proceeded according to strict sauna protocol, sampling each of the seven different types of sauna on offer. These varied from traditional wood smoke to modern electric 'silent' saunas – popular, as you might imagine, with the Finns! – 'talking saunas', dry saunas and those heated to different temperatures were also available. In between, a cool shower was an invigorating tonic.

The nudity aspect of all this didn't bother me – it never really has – but I did have an aversion to really cold water against my skin, probably due to unpleasant memories of outings to open-air baths in Clontarf as a kid. After the sixth sauna, I felt bold enough to venture outside, run fifteen metres or so in the nip, down some steps and take a plunge into the lake, just as the Danish Ambassador had told me she had done the previous week. The first time, it worked without a hitch, though those icy cold lake waters had a similar effect to what I imagine a heart attack would be, intense pain and paralysis. But the after-effect, an indescribably pleasurable, warm glow from tip to toe is almost worth it.

Feeling brave and knowing it was for the last time that evening, after the seventh sauna, I dashed out and down the steps again without fear and with some quiet satisfaction at my bravery. Alas, I had the inevitable fall that comes with such pride. Just as I stepped on to the last metal rung, my right foot slipped and I came down heavily, stumbling and sliding into the water at the same time. The pain this time was more excruciating and quite different, but I managed to haul myself out of the lake and stumble back inside. We then went in for a well-earned supper, beginning with the ubiquitous vodka shot and lots of raw herring, served ten different ways.

I went home that night feeling quite satisfied that I had survived, almost enjoyed, the experience of the Finnish Sauna Society and had lived to tell the tale to my Danish colleague when next we met. My sleep that night was disturbed by occasional twinges but nothing too bad provided I lay on my left side. However, the next morning, I couldn't move. My right side had a searing pain when I tried to roll out of bed. Eventually, after several different techniques, I shuffled my way out of bed in a semi-sliding fashion, landing on both feet. And there I was, stuck, hardly able to move. With Siobhán's assistance, I got dressed and headed slowly into work. By lunchtime, the pain was getting worse every time I tried to walk. There was nothing for it but to head to our local medical clinic, efficient but expensive since as a foreigner I did not have access to the excellent free Finnish medical service.

The doctor immediately referred me to their brilliant physio-therapist. After half an hour of manipulation, he suddenly pressed hard on my left side and with barely a yelp I felt the pain disappear completely. He explained that I had displaced my left pelvic bone as a result of my slip-slide into the water the night before. He said it might take several more manipulations before his efforts stuck and so it proved. Four sessions later, I felt complete again, and not inclined to mention anything to the Dane or to repeat the Sauna Society experience, I spent the remaining two years making up increasingly desperate excuses! The sequel to this embarrassing episode is that four years later I had a further accident involving a herniated disc which required some sophisticated surgery by a brilliant young Irish neurosurgeon, US-trained. I believe the one wouldn't have happened without the other.

Finland also has quite an interesting history. Not only were they not part of the greater Viking network in Scandinavia, but they embraced Sweden for a while or, more correctly, allowed Sweden to embrace them before succumbing to Russian imperial charm in 1809, with the status of Grand Duchy. Indeed, in the heart of old Helsinki, the National Lutheran Cathedral, formerly the Nicholas Cathedral, dominates both the Helsinki skyline and a grand plaza which includes an impressive memorial statue to Czar Alexander II, the only surviving statue of a Russian Czar outside of Russia itself. He gave the Finns greater autonomy and many Finns still admire him, even though he was assassinated in a nearby building by a Finnish nationalist. The story goes that the Czar was badly wounded and bleeding heavily, but an early medical intervention may have saved him. The doctor called to attend him, however, is reported to have dilly-dallied deliberately, for political reasons, thereby allowing the Czar to die.

One of the great heroes of Finnish contemporary history is Carl Gustaf Emil Mannerheim, 1867-1951, Marshal of Finland and saviour of the country from Soviet occupation. One cannot escape, never mind overestimate, the man's influence on Finland as he strode across the stage of early twentieth century history. Mannerheim was born into a family of noble Swedish origin who settled in Finland in the eighteenth century; his forebears made and lost a lot of money, most of it gambled away by his father who also subsequently abandoned his mother and her four sons. Mannerheim became a cavalry officer in the Russian Imperial Army and at one point served as personal escort to Czar Nicholas II, shortly before the revolution broke out in St. Petersburg. Mannerheim had a distinguished military career receiving a medal for gallantry on the Eastern Front in World War I. He also led a pioneering expedition from St. Petersburg to Peking in 1906-08. Rumour had it he was tasked with spying for Russia along the way. In the course of his long life, he was a contemporary of Churchill, Hitler, Stalin, Roosevelt, de Gaulle and de Valera. He met Hitler twice, including in 1942 at an airfield in Eastern Finland, near Lake Saimaa and only seven kilometres from the border with Russia, on the occasion of Mannerheim's seventy-fifth birthday. Hitler flew in from Berlin, despite the obvious risk, for a celebratory birthday lunch held nearby. The airfield is still operational today, used by the Finnish Coastguard, its basic mizzen huts hardly changed since its most controversial visitor landed there some 80 years ago.

Mannerheim led the White Finnish forces in the struggle for independence in 1917 and in the short, brutal Civil War that followed. He retired from active politics shortly thereafter, but was brought back at the start of World War II to lead the

Finnish defence forces struggling to keep the Russians at bay in the famous Winter War of 1940. In fact, the Finns provoked the Russians by laying claim to Vyborg in Karelia, a long-disputed border territory in Easter Finland, the heart of Finnish culture. One of the great myth-legends of Finland is that an ill-equipped Russian Bear rolled into Karelia and was sand-bagged by clever hit-and-run guerrilla tactics masterminded by Mannerheim.

However, Mannerheim went on to make a fatal mistake, believing in 1942 that Nazi Germany would win World War II. Succumbing to German pressure, Mannerheim invited German troops onto Finnish soil to help with their border campaign against Soviet Russia. In what is called the Continuation War in Finland, the Russian steamroller pushed both the Finns and the Germans back, losing all territorial gains made in the Winter War and more besides. A recent Finnish film, *The Forgotten Soldier*, is a compelling three-hour visual account of this tragic part of Finnish contemporary history. Helsinki was bombed by Soviet bombers and Mannerheim was threatened with complete occupation of Finland if he did not force the remaining German troops to leave Finland. Again, Finland's army had to turn around and fight the Germans, forcing them out through Lapland into northern Norway in a quick and nasty campaign.

The ultimate price Finland had to pay to avoid Russian occupation in 1944 was to meet an extremely large Reparations bill, overseen by a Russian Commission headquartered in Helsinki after hostilities ended. To pay the Russians, Finland was obliged to set up a number of heavy engineering operations specifically to supply Russia with badly needed post-war industrial equipment. Thus, companies like Wartsila came into being, beginning a major growth period for Finnish heavy industry. Reparations were deemed fully repaid shortly after Stalin's death and many of the firms established in that era went on to become major multinationals. Wartsila, for instance, is a major international employer, supplying one in three of all marine engines in use worldwide, and manufacturing over one per cent of the world's electricity generators. So, ironically, reparations rather than occupation were to the longer-term benefit of Finland as a modern economy, though it would not be until much later that the country started to turn towards the West.

In the meantime, Mannerheim went into retirement and eventually passed away in semi-exile in Switzerland in 1951. But his legend lives on and is still respected. Statues and streets abound with his name and he is once more revered as the Saviour of Finland in its hour of need.

There is a fine Mannerheim Museum in his former Helsinki residence, run by volunteers from the University of Helsinki, full of amazing trophies and artefacts collected during his long life. Some of the most unusual date from the three-year trek he made on a white horse across the steppes and through Mongolia to Peking in the first decade of the twentieth century, as mentioned earlier. He obviously did a lot of hunting along the way!

Another interesting artefact which I spotted in the dining room – he frequently hosted dinner parties for visiting VIPs – was a 1938 Menu Card. The dinner was held to mark the visit of a British Government delegation to Helsinki in an ultimately unsuccessful attempt to keep Finland neutral and out of the impending conflict. The British delegation was led by Robert Vansittart, Permanent Head of the Foreign & Commonwealth office. And it included that controversial Irishman, Brendan Bracken, he of Churchill fame, firstly as a close confidante and advisor and subsequently as Minister for Propaganda during the war itself. Bracken was a product of the Benedictines at Glenstal, though hardly their favourite alumnus, having either run away or been expelled from Glenstal early on. His father was a founding member of the GAA, being present at its inaugural meeting.

Evidently, the notorious Brendan Bracken charm did not captivate old Mannerheim who was a Germanophile. Had Bracken had his way that night, perhaps the subsequent history of Finland – and Europe – could have been fundamentally altered.

The apocryphal story circulates that Mannerheim's post-war visit to de Gaulle in Paris to receive an honorary Legion d'Honneur in exchange for its Finnish counterpart, the White Cross, nearly ended in disaster when Mannerheim turned up in full regalia of Marshal of Finland to present de Gaulle with the White Iron Cross insignia, whose chain was made up of Swastika-like links. The Swastika had been in use as a popular symbol in Finland since the early 1930s, appearing on building designs as an architectural flourish, as part of the ancient national folk-tale, *The Kalevala*, and even as the official marking on Finnish Air Force aeroplanes and uniforms. Hence, it had also been used as a symbol in the highest national award.

De Gaulle is said to have frowned heavily when the White Cross and chain were put over his long neck. He immediately pulled up the collars of his own uniform to cover the chain so that it no longer showed in the official photographs of the occasion. Franco-Finnish relations took a long time to recover! Eventually, the Swastika was replaced on the chain by a more politically acceptable link, though both the Mannerheim Museum and the Air Force Museum still have the symbol on display for those who might notice it.

One of my great pleasures was to visit the small eastern town of Mikkeli which was the base for Mannerheim and his General Staff during the Winter War (1940) and Continuation War (1942-44). While there, touting for business opportunities and linkages between Irish and Finnish SMEs, I was entertained by the Mayor at the Mikkeli Club, the original HQ for Mannerheim and his General Staff, full of black and white photos from the period. It was like going back in time to 1940, a magical experience. We replicated the traditional toast to Finland with the Marshal's own brand Schnapps, which he insisted should be drunk by his officers assembled every day with a steady hand, shot glass filled to the brim and with just three sips to empty it.

The logic was that any officer less than fully fit, both mentally and physically, would betray himself by any shake in his hand. It wasn't as easy as it sounded; and clever branding or not, the Marshal's own Schnapps tasted particularly good on that occasion! Other Mannerheim delights included visits to see his personal train carriage used during the war, now sitting on a siding in Mikkeli, and to the former war-time wooden army barracks, now a museum to Mannerheim's war campaigns. All in all, Mikkeli is well worth a detour.

Another place I enjoyed visiting was the lake region of Saimaa, the fourth largest in Europe, a lacework of large and small waters, interconnected and intertwined like a spider's web. At one end was probably the most scenic city in Finland, Kuopio, home to Thousand Island Drive, reminiscent of some US idyllic suburb. Kuopio was also home to an innovative science park. At its other end of the lake lay the city of Lappeenranta, again a stunning location and hub border crossing point into Finnish Russia (also known as Eastern Karelia). Lappeenranta had a bigger duty free revenue than Helsinki as many Russians invested in beautiful lakeside properties. The city was one of the worst affected areas in Finland by the sanctions and counter-sanctions regimes of the EU and Russia over the Crimea and Ukraine. Lappeenranta is home to an excellent University of Technology with a nearly 30 per cent foreign student population, mainly Chinese. And last but not least, Lappeenranta is linked by a canal to the spiritual heart of Finland, Russian occupied since 1945, the city of Vyburg, formerly Vipuri.

I was taken on a visit to the Russian border by the Finnish Coast Guard who are responsible for the external borders of Finland. We went by Sikorski helicopter, itself a thrilling experience! We touched down at the tiny, isolated airstrip I mentioned, Imatra. There was something spooky about that experience, knowing the Nazi dictator and war criminal had stood on the same apron as we were on. Nearby, deep in the forest and overgrown by 90 years of vegetation, is a large ski-jump, once well inside Finland and the site of pre-war winter games, now literally with a line of border markers running along its slide bed.

We were twenty or so foreign Heads of Mission on that overnight border visitation, all encouraged to participate in the strictly segregated sauna ritual. Looking back, it was quite amusing to see all these pot-bellied, grey haired old men of various shapes and sizes, representatives of big powers and small, lanky Nordics and tubby Mediterraneans alike, all standing around sipping beer or water in between nipping (literally) in and out of the extremely hot sauna, with only a casually draped towel to preserve their modesty. Our National Day reception encounters were never quite the same after that!

And over a well-earned dinner afterwards, I started what turned into a highly charged sing-song, as each Ambassador did their party piece. 'Molly Malone' was a universal favourite with a rousing chorus by all to rival 'Amhrán na bhFiann'. The Finns at the dinner, a Coast Guard Admiral and his deputy, surprised us all by their rowdy renditions of some dubious shanties fortunately sung in Finnish to the accompaniment of lots of rude gestures. Finns can be fun when they want to be!

It was shortly after that most interesting visit that Finland, complacent up to then and reliant on Russian diligence in sealing off the border from their side, began to experience an influx of incursions from economic migrants who had made their way from the Mediterranean up through Russia to the Finnish border.

Finland lays claim to be the real home of Santa Claus, though Norway may dispute this. Certainly, the home village of this iconic figure is located just to the north of the Arctic Circle city of Rovaniemi in a rather disappointing Santa Village cluster just off a main road; they might at least have built it much deeper into the expansive forest that surrounded it. Of course, I had to meet Santa. After all, he had visited me so many times in the past it was the least I could do.

And I did meet him, and he was first class! He remembered me, where I lived and the many, many presents he had brought me, especially when I was an only child, before my sisters appeared on the scene. On the way out, I had a meeting with his boss, the Village Managing Director. I patiently explained about the St. Patrick's Day 'Greening' initiative and suggested it would be a publicity coup if Santa were to consent to turn both himself and his surroundings green for one day of the year, especially as 17 March was his quiet season. On my way out, I also had a sleigh ride pulled by a real reindeer which was fun, too!

On my return to Helsinki I duly reported my initiative to the young lady who was the Tourism Ireland rep. based in Stockholm. She seemed a bit stunned by the thought of a green Santa but began to see the potential. This could, in fact, be something special, reviving what had become a slightly overdone campaign. Alas, it was not to be. I heard later in the year, shortly after I had retired, that Santa Village Inc. had gone bankrupt, not due to a lack of young customers, but due to a bad investment decision by its owners. A shame for sure; I am still convinced Father Christmas in an emerald green woolly suit would have made headlines worldwide!

My favourite place in Finland has to be the Turku Archipelago, an endless cluster of big and small islands stretching far into the Baltic to the southwest of Turku, Finland's original Swedish-speaking capital city. One can drive, in theory, from Turku to Mariehamn, the capital of the Åland Islands, which are almost within touching distance of the Swedish archipelago. In practice, it is easier either to fly to Mariehamn or to go via the ever-popular ferry service network.

Åland once was populated by Swedes, including Swedish Vikings in their day, but centuries later lost their claim to the islands to the Russian Empire in the war of 1808. After World War I and Finland's independence, the League of Nations was asked to arbitrate between Sweden and Finland over rival claims to the islands. The islanders themselves wanted to revert to Swedish hegemony but in typical League fashion for getting disputes wrong, the Åland Islands ended up as an autonomous region of Finland. It is also, unusually, a demilitarised zone. The islands have a population of 25,000, operate strict residency regulations and Åland is the richest place in Finland, beneficiary of a national tax redistribution system which returns generous subsidies to keep the locals onside.

They also have a noble history as seafarers, with their own ocean-going fleet of sailing clippers which rivalled most other maritime nations for much of the nineteenth and early twentieth centuries. Now, alas, only a fine Mariehamn Maritime Museum and an endless stream of ferries between Finland and Sweden denote their sea supremacy. But there is another reason Åland is such a popular port of call. The designation of Åland as an autonomous territory has meant that it can operate as a duty free zone inside the European Union, yet another marvellous anomaly, among many, Brussels chooses to ignore.

The ferry companies have it down to a fine art. With a capacity of over 2,000 passengers, mostly full every day, the ferries literally slow down as they reach Mariehamn, do a quick spin around, back into the tiny harbour dock, lower their stern doors for all of five minutes, then are up and away in no time. I witnessed this at midnight on the way out to Stockholm, and at about 4.00 am in the morning on the return journey. This allows them to stock their on-board shops, which are the entire length of the ship and laid out like a mini-shopping mall, with a plethora of booze and tobacco and perfumes and candies of all kinds and varieties, all duty free. In other words, Finland and Sweden have literally exploited a giant-sized excise loophole that is the envy of the rest of the European Union. Perhaps, we will get our own back with Brexit? Holyhead revived?

Siobhán and myself also had the particular pleasure of being guests of Seppo Romana, a remarkable business entrepreneur cum psychologist who had purchased a former rescue vessel, *Outoori*, which literally means 'rescue' in Finnish, and had faithfully restored it at great personal expense. It was an ugly duckling of a boat, its shape reminiscent of a rubber duck, but after its renovation it was very comfortable inside and we had several pleasant summer cruises around the Turku Archipelago with Captain Romana at the wheel.

It was fun to island-hop and to sleep on board and since Seppo and his spouse were accomplished chefs in their own right we also dined well. I provided the wine. And there was the nightly sauna routine, strictly segregated in Finnish fashion, and with many a good discussion in between icy Baltic plunges (yes, I was cautious about getting in and out after my traumatic Sauna Society experience). And everywhere we went, despite her waddle-like appearance, *Outoori* drew respect from other sailors as she was known as 'the old rescue boat' which had saved many lives during her distinguished Baltic rescue career.

It is that aspect of Finland that I liked so much – preservation of venerable artefacts rather than giving in to a disposable, bling society culture that has become so prevalent elsewhere. Finns are a shy, modest people. Like Canadians, they enjoy the pleasures of a simple, outdoor existence, communing with nature, in among the trees and alongside water whenever possible – which it often is in a country of a hundred thousand lakes. They preserve as much of their family and social traditions as they can, passed down from one generation to the next, with family country dwellings, often quite basic log structures, held in trust for future generations. I love the continuity. I love the history. I love the respect for nature.

Even in their large cities, many brought to ruin during the World War II campaigns, the architecture is simple, practical, that is, with their climate factored in, solid and unadorned. Neon lighting and gaudy shop fronts and signage are not for Finnish enterprises. One has to look hard, sometimes, to distinguish between a shop and private residence. Finns are not at all 'showy' or vulgar, certainly not exhibitionist, except, perhaps, in the sauna!

And they do appreciate the good things of life. One of the Embassy's most active contacts was Matti Raty, the President of the Friends of Irish Whiskey, which in five years has grown to a membership of some 500. Matti has twice organised visits to Ireland for some 50 people for a week's tour of Irish distilleries. Not too many individuals can match that claim to fame!

Perhaps my only criticism of the Finns is that they guard their privacy jealously and do not communicate with neighbours except in a formal, quite distant manner. One classic example is how they handle death and funerals. The spouse of the Finnish Irish Business Club Secretary, a lovely lady with no discernible health problems, died suddenly in her sleep due to an undiagnosed heart issue. I had been sitting beside her at a dinner party only the week before. We had met many times at club occasions in the previous year. Yet the news of her passing came via one of the Finnish secretaries in the office who had read the announcement in the newspaper. Fair enough.

My immediate reaction was to jump in the car and go to comfort my bereaved friend. But no, I was told that is not the Finnish way. No one gathers at the house except close family. Even then, it takes three to four weeks before the burial can take place. And all that happens, even to those of a Lutheran persuasion, is a simple, strictly family only service on the day of interment. Others such as neighbours, even old friends, are not encouraged to turn up. One may buy an outsized funeral card and have it delivered on the day instead. Otherwise, funerals in Finland are very private affairs, and grief is not expressed openly. I bent if not broke the rules by eventually calling in on my friend after about 10 days and before the burial ceremony. In the event, he seemed very touched and I did not feel he had been offended by this breach of protocol.

Seamus Heaney visited Finland in the 1980s, prior to writing *North*. One of his close friends was Dr. Anthony Johnson, Professor of English Literature at Abu University in Turku, the oldest Swedish-speaking university in the country. Seamus died tragically shortly after my arrival in Helsinki, so one of my first official acts was to attend a memorial event organised by Anthony in September, 2013.

I learnt that Seamus had intended to revisit Finland and early preparations for his visit were in hand when he passed away. Sadly, it was not to be, as it would have been a great honour. Anthony told me after the tribute to Seamus that he had already received some unpublished material from him in anticipation of his next visit. So we can expect some hitherto unpublished Heaney writings to appear sometime in the not too distant future.

Anthony himself is an amazingly accomplished musician, composer, violinist and all-round musical talent. He is a regular participant at the Irish Festival of Oulu, a small city just outside the Arctic Circle on the Gulf of Ostrobothnia, the northern limit of the Baltic Sea. It was, until quite recently, home to a significant number of Nokia employees, many of whom were Irish. Sad to say, that arm of Nokia was subsumed into Microsoft and dismantled, leaving many unemployed with little alternative opportunities. Some moved elsewhere, others stayed.

Coincidentally, a New York Irish American, a musician, had married a Finn and they had moved back to her home city of Oulu, of which more anon. It is very much the norm for Finnish females to bring their male partners home to Finland where they end up, in a variation on the Viking theme of carrying off foreign women as slaves and concubines, as home husbands, Few are able to speak the Finnish language, which can take years to learn, and since Finns speak such good English, even with the famous hesitancy of that icon of our economic ruin, Olli Rehn, few Irish people make the effort to learn it.

And Finns, like many other small nations, can be quite critical of those who attempt to speak Finnish. They do not appreciate trying on the *cúpla focail*, so beloved of visitors to Ireland. And those foolish enough to persist invariably make horrific mistakes since Finnish is very much an oral, guttural, soft-spoken, swallowed language where pronunciation and inflection are paramount. Beware, you were warned!

In any event, I quickly gave up asking Irish men I met in Finland what had brought them there. It was invariably a Finnish woman. And while some had prospered in their new environment, others, handicapped by linguistic obstacles, had had to do with rather modest means of support for their family units. We did, of course, have several start-up entrepreneurs, agronomists and even a wood-working genius among our Irish community, and even a few professional musicians. I may name names anon.

But back to Oulu and the Irish Festival, which was started in 2005, when times were still good locally, by one Brent Cassidy, or Brent O'Caseide, as he preferred to be known. Brent was the

Irish American mentioned above. His parents were New York Irish American and he loved Ireland, its music and culture, and he was also a talented musician. He taught himself the Irish language and visited the Donegal Gaeltacht every year. He would while away the long, dark winters in Northern Finland by playing his bodhran and whistle and eventually decided he would like to share his joy of all things Irish by organising an Irish cultural event once a year in October. Thus, the Oulu Irish Festival was born. Brent convinced the local authority to assist with the finances and soon had a successful 50:50 public-private partnership sponsorship in place.

The festival has gone from strength to strength, a week-long fest of Irish musicians (there were fifty-six at the festival I attended in 2013), authors and poets, stage actors, seannachai, dancers and so on, and the University of Oulu, site of the Marti Atassari Centre for International Studies, provided a platform for an annual lecture on an Irish topic (I gave one in 2016 on Ireland's 1916). The festival, despite being located only 200 kilometres from the Arctic Circle, is now the largest Irish cultural event in the Nordic Baltic region and has become an established date on the international Irish music circuit. For its tenth anniversary in 2015, The Chieftains even made an appearance, a great tribute to Brent's organisational prowess and tenacity.

And Oulu is also famous for being the site of the 'Most northerly game of Gaelic Football in the world'. A Google search will take you to a clip of two teams shivering under stadium lights as the Oulu Irish Elks played the Helsinki Harps, with yours truly throwing in the ball and awarding the Finland GAA Challenge Cup, a rather impressive trophy in its own right.

I never imagined in my wildest dreams that I would be witness to such an unusual game of Gaelic sport! It is a credit to all those concerned that GAA established itself in the Nordics a number of years ago. When I arrived in Helsinki in 2013 we had one team, the Harps. By the time I left two years later, we had seven men's teams throughout the country, two women's teams and a growing youth wing. Not all the participants were of Irish as we had Brazilians, Portuguese, Scots and a few Russians and Finns togging out. I am proud to say that I was able to encourage these endeavours by various means and that at my farewell reception I was presented with a Harps jersey, a major honour.

I am next going to recount one of the many amazing coincidences that have come my way over 40 years in the Irish Diplomatic Service. I now believe that coincidence is, in fact, part of our karma, that our spirit is inexplicably complex, much more so than we can imagine, and that coincidence is part of a pre-determined pattern laid out for each individual ... but enough philosophy.

One of my first sorties outside Helsinki was to Tampere, 'the Manchester of Finland', the second largest city after Helsinki, located in central Finland and host to considerable textile and pottery industries in the mid-nineteenth century. The city was also the scene of a major battle between the White and Red sides in the Civil War, and Mannerheim prevailed over the Communist Finnish forces after an epic campaign.

The industrial heart of Tampere has been totally revamped in a sensitive way, the old red brick mills and warehouses converted into galleries and shops, the large weir channel linking the upper and lower lakes now a scenic cycleway running through the city centre. What has been achieved by the town planners in preserving the best in a delicate transformation is wonderful to behold and a model for other cities.

Tampere was also the location of one of my final official acts, one in which I am extremely proud of playing my part.

In early 2015, I received a letter from a school teacher in Tampere, an Irishman married, of course, to a Finn and happily promoting his Irish heritage among his pupils and staff colleagues. Charles Harkin bounced off me an idea he had for his twelfth grade class in Tammela School to translate the Irish Proclamation of 1916 into Finnish, something that had not been done before (though it was later discovered that a Finn and a Swede, sailors from a ship docked in Dublin Port, had walked as far as the GPO and offered to fight for the rebel cause. This they did, welcomed with open arms by Pearse and Connolly; one was wounded, they were briefly interned, then sent on their way).

I jumped at the idea and promised my full support. It would be a fitting tribute to the men and women of 1916, one of whom was my maternal grandfather, Edward Tuke, Volunteer No. 79 in the Irish Citizen Army. I contacted HQ and was linked through to the 1916-2016 Coordinator in the Department of Defence. He, too, was thrilled and immediately informed his committee, suggesting that one aspect of the commemorations should be foreign language translations of the proclamation, though I never saw any attention being given to this during the anniversary celebrations in which I participated during 2016; perhaps, the powers-that-be had second thoughts.

In any event, the Tammela School children, including several of non-Finnish ethnic origin, did a brilliant job. I attended the school to accept officially a framed copy of the 1916 Proclamation in Finnish and was given a rousing welcome by the entire school, every one of the 800 assembled waving small Irish tricolour flags. I have a wonderful series of photos to prove it.

I then invited Charles to bring the class to pay a visit to the official residence of the Irish Ambassador to Finland where I organised an Irish food and drinks reception for them. Bravo Tammela, bravo Charles! It was a proud moment and the legacy endures.

I also had the pleasure of meeting one of the longest serving members of the Irish community resident in Finland, Roger Luke, who moved to Tampere in the 1960s to take up a lecturing post in the English Department at the University of Tampere, one of Finland's major academic institutions and with a specialism in foreign languages. In more recent years, Roger had been teaching a specific course on Irish Studies and always invited the Ambassador up to give a talk on modern Ireland.

I was delighted to follow in my predecessors' footsteps. However, my curiosity was immediately heightened by his name. A memory came to me that my Dad, who moved in advertising circles in Dublin, and my favourite Uncle Fintan (Tuke), who did likewise, both had a good mutual friend in a Dave Luke who ran a small trade publications business and who lived on the Rathgar Road. I would occasionally be hauled along to say hello – I was ten or eleven at the time. I remember a large house, messy, chaotic and filled with thick clouds of cigarette smoke. Dave was 'a character', a bit of a rascal, and I think both Dad and Fintan had a soft spot for him and tried to help him out from time to time in his dubious family circumstances.

Lo and behold, when Roger strode in to meet me for the first time, I felt I had been hit by that self-same memory right between the eyes. Roger, a slight character in his sixties, said

'Hello Ambassador' and I replied 'You *are* Dave Luke's son!' He asked how I could possibly know that and I said that he was the spitting image of his father. It was like meeting Dave's ghost! They even had the same tone of voice as I recalled it, though Roger was more upright in character and didn't smoke at all.

I had never met Roger before; he had been away at university (Trinity, as it happens) and our paths had not crossed. I didn't even know of his existence back then. So, coincidence or karma? On its own, perhaps the former, but as a pattern through my life, more like fate and spirit.

I also found out that Roger had been in the habit of calling to the embassy to collect back issues of *The Irish Times* so that confirmed his family credentials! Roger became a firm friend and was very helpful in organising a number of visits to Tampere for me, to the university and to major sites around the city, including the magnificent Lutheran art nouveau-period cathedral built in the early 1900s.

Unusually for a Lutheran place of worship, it contains an impressive amount of decoration, with some of the finest homo-erotic fresco art I have ever seen, carried out by a famous Finnish artist, Hugo Simberg; they so shocked the congregation at first that the church had to be kept locked outside service hours. Most important of all, though, is the national treasure by Simberg, the world famous *The Wounded Angel*, a watercolour like fresco whose canvas equivalent is in pride of place at the National Gallery of Finland's Athenaeum gallery in the centre of Helsinki. It portrays a young female-like angel with a bandage around her head being carried on a stretcher by two boy chimney sweeps. It is stunning!

With Roger's help, I also organised a day seminar and exhibition on the cooperation between Finland and Ireland in UN peacekeeping which goes back some 50 years now and whose most recent example is the highly effective UNIFIL Battalion which is half Irish, half Finnish with a rotating command structure. For this occasion, I had deliberately wanted to spread our influence outside of Helsinki, the traditional location. Tampere University also hosted a Centre for Peace Studies on campus so it seemed the ideal place to pitch our tent.

I was delighted that both the Irish Secretary General of the Department of Defence and his Deputy and their Finnish equivalents took part, as did Col. Howard Berney, then Deputy Commander of the EU Nordic Task Force, based in Stockholm. Howard, it turned out, is married to one of the Finnegan siblings who runs Dalkey's most famous pub, and my beloved local, Finnegan's Sorrento, dating from 1927. Finnegan's neighbour and frequent customers were our close friend Maeve Binchy and her spouse, Gordon, who is hale and hearty and still an occasional visitor there. Bono, another local, also appears from time to time, though I have never bumped into him there (I did in Portland, Oregon, however).

And in 2015 Michelle Obama and her two daughters had lunch in Finnegan's as his guests. Siobhán was down in the village (no, Dalkey is *not* a town) that day and heard the rumour that they were about to arrive. She joined a small crowd opposite the pub entrance and a few minutes later, a convoy of black vans appeared, screeched to a halt and their passengers were ushered inside at great speed. Half an hour later, the same occurred in reverse order. Obviously, Michelle wasn't in the mood to greet her local fans!

Despite the VIPness of its reputation, Finnegan's retains the cosy atmosphere, inside and out, of your typical early twentieth century hostelry, and long may it continue.

Another place Roger led me to in Tampere was O'Connell's Irish Bar, just opposite Tampere train station. Not quite as snug as Finnegan's but it was the only genuine Irish pub, owned by Simon from Ireland who also pulled an excellent pint of Guinness there. There was a snug where once a week, Roger and his students would gather for social intercourse. I enjoyed it so much I made it a regular item on my future visits. For a few brief moments I was beamed back to the Trinity Buttery and the glorious cut and trust of intellectual sparring. Great fun.

And Finland was fun! That's what made it the best final posting I could have wished for. Finns occasionally get a bad press, not least from Monty Python & Co., but they deserve much more sympathetic consideration for creating a decent society in a challenging environment.

So I was working normally on Friday August 14, retired on Saturday August 15 and unpacking boxes from a lifetime of moving about on Monday August 17 ...

Since then ...

I came home and campaigned, ultimately with success and to the benefit of future generations of Irish civil servants, for the removal of mandatory retirement at 65. Now you can go on, under certain conditions, until you are 70. That of course does not prevent or preclude those who wish to retire at an earlier age from doing so.

Siobhán came home with me but has continued to work as a copy editor, with good success. She had the great misfortune to shatter her heel on her weekly hike only three weeks after moving home, and a week later fell off a stool and broke her wrist. The following months laid waste to our retirement planning!

Since then, we have visited the land of Oz, that lucky country, as often as possible to spend time with our children there, Barry and his spouse Aisling and son James, and Andrea and her husband, Mark, and Arpad and Audrey, and seeing our special friends there, too, such as 'Mary B', sister of my old and close friend and colleague, the legendary Joe Brennan (known to every diplomat who has ever served in Dublin), and Rosemary Sheehan and husband, Gavan.

In between, and as a result of those disruptive visits as I call them, I have learnt a lot, especially from establishing, with the help of a remarkable lady, Annie Johnston, a local group in Dun Laoghaire of U3A, the University of the Third Age, which I first came across in Hawthorn, a suburb of Melbourne. Our group here, serving Dun Laoghaire, Dalkey and Killiney, now has some 200 members after only three years in existence, and there are three spin-off groups in Monkstown, Bray and Greystones, all of similar size. The thirst for knowledge is not abated by age.

So, I will finish as I started, by reciting a toast I learnt off many years ago and which has brought me great pleasure and some praise from its recipients:

> There are good ships,
> There are wood ships,
> there are ships that sail the sea
> But the best ships are FRIENDships
> And may they always be!

Afterword

Looking back, a list of some interesting times I have lived through might include:

Early memories of the Soviet tanks on the streets of Budapest, 1956. Sputnik, 1957, which started the 'Space Race' and Yuri Gagarin's single space orbit, 1961.

Flying, for the first time, in a DC 3; a kind Finnish friend took me on a DC 3 memorial flight in 2014 and the thrill was just as great!

In my formative teenage years, JFK's assassination, 22 November, 1963 (I was at home in Sanderstead when the news broke; I also recall sitting on my Uncle Fintan's shoulders when the JFK motorcade swept down Parliament Street near City Hall) and his brother Robert's tragic demise in June 1968 (I was driving through the Kent countryside at the time), are still searingly painful memories of man's inhumanity to man.

And the passing of Pope John XXIII was also a very sad loss for Roman Catholics at a critical period of reform. It was never the same again.

British politics, from Macmillan through Wilson, Thatcher, Blair and beyond has been an enduring fascination, no more so than in its most recent manifestation, Brexit. Likewise, Ireland's membership of the European Union, now fast approaching 50 years, was seminal to my life experiences.

Walking on the moon, 9/11, the internet, advances in medicine, population explosion, the callous degradation of our environment – so many interesting issues and curiosities in such a short period, almost too many to mention, certainly here.

It has been a privilege to live in such a splendid, multicoloured and cultural era. Thank you, God! Amen!

PS: Mother Nature has visited the Covid 19 pandemic upon us all; she is taking her revenge on overpopulation and environmental abuse, harsh but inevitable.

Index